THE MANDARIN WAY

THE
MANDARIN
WAY

by Cecilia Sun Yun Chiang

as told to Allan Carr

AN ATLANTIC MONTHLY PRESS BOOK

Little, Brown and Company — Boston – Toronto

SECOND PRINTING

T 03/74

Frontispiece photograph by Harris of Romaine

Photograph used throughout book: "Waiting for Guests by Lamplight," from the
Collection of the National Palace Museum, Taipei, Taiwan, Republic of China

Library of Congress Cataloging in Publication Data

Chiang, Cecilia Sun Yun.
    The Mandarin way.

    "An Atlantic Monthly Press book."
    1. China--Social life and customs. 2. Cookery,
Chinese. I. Carr, Allan. II. Title.
DS721.C48127 1974   394.1'0951   73-16127
ISBN 0-316-13900-9

ATLANTIC—LITTLE, BROWN BOOKS
ARE PUBLISHED BY
LITTLE, BROWN AND COMPANY
IN ASSOCIATION WITH
THE ATLANTIC MONTHLY PRESS

Published simultaneously in Canada by Little, Brown & Company (Canada)
Limited
PRINTED IN THE UNITED STATES OF AMERICA

To the memory of my mother
Sun Shueh Yun-hwei
who showed me the way
all her life

為軫念先　慈生平訓
誨鞠育之劬勞謹以
本書獻奉吾　母在天
之靈

無錫

江孫芸敬誌癸丑年
元月

Introduction

How does one bring back the past, without letters or documents, remembering in an alien land? When I first thought of gathering this book together, I was puzzled by the problems, which also included the difficulty of expressing the word associations of one culture in the language of another. And yet, as I began to talk to Allan Carr, the memories flooded in, question and answer led backward into the past. Fortunately I have a reliable memory, trained in the Chinese fashion, and exercising it in our conversations has prompted me to recall what I might have overlooked, just as his questions have sometimes suggested details which I might not have thought of interest. The way of life I have set out to recapture no longer exists. The last ten years have completed its destruction: yet since my family background and the path of my life have given me unusual opportunities of knowing both the manner of living of the Mandarin classes and of the Chinese people at large in the first half of this century, I believe there may be others who will find interest in exploring the same road.

The reader will discover that I have devoted a good deal of space to the banquets and festivals of the Chinese calendar and the foods associated with the changing seasons of the year. And there are several good reasons for this. In the first place, we Chinese love to eat. The moment of mealtimes is always a happy family reunion, often noisy and informal, and only the most ceremonious occasion calls for a strict etiquette and decorum. In a household such as I knew as a child, numbering rarely fewer than twenty people and constantly enlarged by random visits from relations, it was always necessary to have a greater supply of food than was needed for the use of the immediate family. Again, both my parents were connoisseurs of good food: my mother from a practical standpoint, and my father as a gourmet. I myself, having enjoyed the many schools of Chinese cuisine at first hand, and now directing my own restaurant in San Francisco, have more than a passing appreciation of the cooking of my homeland. For these reasons Allan Carr and I have alternated chapters of personal reminiscence with interludes in which passages about food are followed by recipes for dishes that I think adapt well to Occidental meals.

Books on Chinese cooking are now legion; and they all tend to suggest that if one follows the directions, success is assured. Chinese dishes are easy to prepare? Nothing could be further from the truth, for although, as in all great cuisines of the world, some dishes have the perfection of simplicity, others require days of preparation and great knowledge and dexterity in the execution.

It may seem surprising to Western ears to hear that Chinese gourmets seldom if ever cook: their knowledge is acquired by watching and eating. In the same way, an apprentice cook in China never receives formal lessons; he is obliged to watch and learn. And one of his first acquired skills, if the Number One cook thinks he is ready, is to learn how to use a cleaver. Cutting, chopping, slicing and skinning form so much a part of the art of preparation that they must be thoroughly understood. The Chinese belief in matching ingredients also means that foods in a dish must always be of the same shape and size —a wise insurance of equal cooking—although, of course, they are not necessarily cooked all at once, since they usually vary in the length of time required. With this preamble, it may be better understood why, even as late as 1949, I had never cooked anything myself, although I had eaten and been exposed to the finest cuisines all my life.

In Shanghai I had an admirable cook, a woman who had an immense repertoire in the Shanghai style and always served up something different at each meal. Japan, however, where I lived with my husband during the occupation by the American forces, was a different story. We had Japanese maids, who spoke neither Cantonese nor Mandarin, and household spices and provisions were in extremely short supply. We Chinese had the advantage of special rations for such things as coffee and could buy from the PX and commissary, but meat, for instance, was extremely expensive. No pigs were raised—they had to be imported from Taiwan—and chickens were small and costly, as much as three United States dollars. The supplies most readily available locally were turnips of all kinds, seafood and pickled vegetables, including seaweed, so that our diet was an odd combination of Japanese and Western styles. Beef was uniformly good—the Kobe beef which has had so much publicity since the war—but the Chinese longed for some of their own food.

One Chinese restaurant there was, near the Chinese Mission, but it was so small, no more than a shack, that dining there always meant a long wait; and in wintertime it was so cold that people often stayed huddled up in their cars until their turn came. They did wait, however—at least the cook was from China. We did not go there all the time as it was so crowded; and fortunately I managed to acquire another maid who had been in Shanghai and spoke that dialect, and whom I could therefore train to prepare the dishes I liked. In the meantime, one of my first cousins, a refugee from Hong Kong, joined with me and a group of friends to open a Chinese restaurant in Tokyo, in the neighborhood of Washington Heights, near the Meiji Shrine. We brought over good cooks from Hong Kong and were amazed at the immediate demand, not only from our own people, but from the Japanese, who were enthusiastic about the food, although at that time only the wealthy could afford it. The restaurant was, in consequence, an immediate success, and the clientele grew and grew. At first, the restaurant had seating for two hundred; after building on additions upstairs, it accommodated four hundred with the cocktail lounge. Our Number One cook became famous for preparing shark fin and eventually he stayed on in Japan and opened a restaurant of his own.

At that time, immediately after the capitulation, men were scarce in Japan and nearly all services in Tokyo and elsewhere were operated by women, even the fire department and the police. Dishwashing, operating elevators, street sweeping, deep-sea diving—every category of work from the lightest to the heaviest—called for women. It was, for the time being, a woman's world, although not designed for their convenience; and I was always struck by the fact that the Japanese man went out to dine with other men at a restaurant or geisha house and drank to excess, whereas our Chinese custom was to go out as a family and remain temperate.

For as long as I stayed in Japan I ate well—and profited by it. When I left in 1961 and went to San Francisco at the urgent call of a widowed sister, I had never thought to open a restaurant again. Nevertheless, I was once more persuaded by a number of friends to take over an establishment on Polk Street, whose owner wanted to sell. The partners who had cajoled me now opted out, and I found myself alone. I decided to serve northern Chinese dishes, which provoked an adverse reaction from my sisters and my friends, who said, "You are wasting your time. People here don't even know what true Cantonese food is—chop suey is all they know!"

Against this chorus of dissent I pursued my plan and had the good fortune to repeat my original Tokyo success. In 1968 I moved my restaurant, The Mandarin, to its present site in Ghirardelli Square, overlooking San Francisco Bay: and now northern Chinese restaurants proliferate all over San Francisco and indeed all across the United States, even when their owners may have been no nearer China than Brooklyn or North Beach. And let me say, as a last introductory comment, that there is no such thing as "Mandarin" cuisine. The cuisine of the Mandarin classes was a combination of the cuisine of the capital, augmented by the specialties of every province: the finest produce, from the limitless resources of the whole of China, prepared by chefs whose skill had been handed down from time immemorial.

Contents

FIRST MOON

THERE WERE NO RED EGGS sent out on my first birthday. A child is one year old at birth in China. If a boy, his birth is an occasion for celebration, a feast, with presents of eggs dyed red sent out by the happy parents to signify the continuance of the family. Since I was a girl, with twelve brothers and sisters, rejoicing at my birth was naturally subdued, and at first my horizon was limited to the courtyards of our house in Peking, where in the earliest years I knew more of my *amah* —my wet nurse—than my parents.

In the late nineteen-twenties Peking consisted of rows and rows of very narrow streets, crossing at right angles, with the Forbidden City as its center. Some of the streets were so narrow that they did not allow the passage of even a sedan chair or rickshaw. The houses and roofs were gray, in sharp contrast to the red walls and blue and yellow tiled roofs of the Imperial palaces. Of this outer world at first I knew little. My parents' house was unlike the majority. It had been an old palace, to the east of the city—the most fashionable quarter —belonging to a historic personage, Shih K'o-fa, chief minister to one of the last Emperors of the Ming dynasty, after whom the street was named—Shih Chia Hu-t'ung (Shih Family Street)—and was arranged in seven rows of buildings separated by courtyards. A distinctive mark of such palaces was the row of stalls for carriages outside the entrance; and whereas most streets consisted of bare earth, the one outside our house was paved with blocks of stone. There was an enormous doorway, with steps on either side and a ramp in the center for the wheels of carriages; beyond was the entrance proper, guarded by a block of stone that could be raised by rings to admit the carriages. In the outer entrance poor people would often take shelter at night. To one side of the doorway, which had big gates with brass knockers in the shape of tiger heads, was the guardroom. At night, the guard beat out the time on a wooden clapper and kept alert for any ill-intentioned prowlers.

The first row of buildings housed the menservants, and the seventh and last, the maidservants, as well as the kitchen and storage area. Around each courtyard was a corridor or veranda, with bamboo curtains which could be let down to keep out the noonday heat. Each courtyard was arranged as a formal garden, with flowerbeds raised above the ground and so constructed that one could sit on their edge, as on a garden seat; and there were large pots with seasonal flowers: the time of the blossoming of the peonies, with their delicate perfume, was especially treasured. In the cool of a summer evening, after dinner, everyone sought the courtyards to eat little delicacies while "catching the summer breeze" (ch'en-liang).

The garden of the palace was not, however, encompassed by this succession of courtyards. It was in the adjoining building, which had only about three rooms and a kitchen and was used as a guesthouse. A little path meandered through the garden, which had a fantastic ornamental rock, or as we call it, a "man-made hill," with nooks and crevices in which we loved to hide. There were also little trees in tubs, and large jars of goldfish. In the center of the garden was an octagonal pavilion, or pa-chiao t'ing, an open pagoda raised a little above the ground with benches around it inside, where in summer one could play mah jong and drink tea. (There are

4

two similar pavilions on Coal Hill, in the Forbidden City, like twin sisters). A moon gate led from the garden into the main house so that guests could either join the family or live quite separately.

Every room in the main house had old-fashioned brick *k'ang*, the beds which could be heated with log fires from beneath. My parents did not like these, for even when covered with thick quilted felt blankets in several layers they remained very hard. Instead they had four-poled brass bedsteads with mosquito netting. We children also had brass beds, my three brothers and nine sisters. An old Chinese house such as this usually had no central heating, so there was good reason for the heated *k'ang*. Our house was again an exception: pipes ran from an underground furnace under brick floors which my father afterwards replaced with hardwood. The fire kept one man continually busy until the Japanese occupation made it impossible to get fuel or keep servants. Peking can be extremely cold in wintertime, and wealthy people frequently had fur pillows and fur blankets to huddle up in, and it must be confessed, often retired to bed to smoke opium.

At weekends the family customarily went by train to my parents' country house beyond the Marco Polo Bridge at Ch'ang-hsin Tien, near where the Japanese were to march on the capital in 1937. This was a much more informal life. We owned a large property—the house itself was not ancient, like the one in Peking, but half Chinese and half Western, like a farmhouse—with acres of fruit trees, flowers and vegetables, and a farmyard of animals: pigs, pigeons, chickens and goats. Consequently there was always a good supply of fresh vegetables, changing with the seasons; and the animals were fattened to provide a feast on such an occasion as the New Year Festival.

Although my parents were by this time completely assimilated into the life of Peking, it had not always been so.

5

When I was four years old, they had made the long and relatively perilous journey by train from Wu-hsi, near Shanghai, to the northern capital. There are vast differences between the provinces of China, in climate, terrain and language, and communications are very poor. With few good roads, much mountainous territory, and large rivers dividing the country, the Chinese have made customs out of necessity, and look upon moves, even from one house to another, with dismay. For my parents to leave their own neighborhood and move to Peking was therefore a major undertaking and a singular change in their lives. When my mother first arrived in Peking she did not even speak Mandarin—only her native Wu-hsi dialect—and I think it was out of homesickness that she took such a great interest in cooking, and began to teach our northern cooks the famous dishes of her home province.

It was not until 1945, V-J Day, that I first saw the remains of my parents' house at Wu-hsi. It had been destroyed by the Japanese bombings; there were just three servants' rooms remaining—the rest was a pile of rubble. It was quite modest in size as far as I could tell, with nothing of the magnificence of our Peking house. My father had been of modest means, the youngest son of a distinguished scholar who instructed people of position. He had been married according to tradition, through the offices of a matchmaker, to my mother, who came of a very wealthy family, owning many of the silk, textile and flour mills for which Wu-hsi is noted. My mother had been considered very modern, for when her parents died young she had taken on the responsibility of running the household and superintending the family properties.

My parents were a great contrast. My father, gentle, unambitious and handsome, liked a quiet, domestic life: he liked to concern himself with our nine dogs, seven cats, talking parakeets and singing birds. Our dogs were Pekinese, the small house pets, and also the breed we call "Four Eye"—

Tchai Go—from Mongolia, which are rather like large sheep-dogs and make very good watchdogs. The cats were every-thing from tiger-striped to gray, and black-and-white to pure black—we are not superstitious about black cats in China. My father's name, Sun Lung-kwong, signifies "bright dragon." I think there is some suggestion of my mother's personality in her name, Sun Shueh Yun-hwei (Shueh being her maiden name), as Yun-hwei means "hidden glory." My mother was always very neat and particular—a perfectionist. Apart from her love of good food, she was also an expert at pickling meat and vegetables, and embroidered beautifully. There was al-ways some special embroidery when each daughter married, and for every grandchild, a hat embroidered with solid gold pieces and intricately trimmed with fur. I am told she had been very beautiful when young, and was known for her exquisite clothes, but unlike most Chinese ladies, whose bound feet cannot support much weight, she later became very fat, and was already over fifty when I was born, and therefore had also ceased, according to custom, to wear any make-up.

Most Chinese have a two-character name, as did my parents, but my sisters and I had only one. I was named Sun Yun, Sun being of course the family name, and Yun meaning "flower of the rue," my given name. When I went back to see the house where I was born, in Wu-hsi, I also went to visit the family tomb. Family tombs are always chosen with great care. A geomancer is consulted, the *feng-shui hsien-sheng,* the diviner of "the spirit of wind and water," who decides the auspicious day for the purchase, the correct orientation and the choice of land. A beautiful site is always selected, and ours was no exception: it is located at one end of the T'ai Hu, the largest lake in China, by a grove of pine trees. The lake is so lovely that at the time of the August Moon, people come from far and wide to have moon-viewing parties on sailboats. A chef cooks on board the fresh fish from the lake, and this has a special name of its own, *ch'uan-ts'ai,* or "boat dishes." Another specialty of Wu-hsi which my mother liked to recall was the freshwater shrimp known as "dancing shrimp." These were eaten raw after being dipped in a tangy sauce of preserved bean curd, pepper, soy sauce, coriander and wine. The shrimp had to be kept in a covered bowl or they would jump out and escape. Barbecued spareribs were another delicious dish which my mother took with her to Peking, although above all, I think my favorite as a child was the way she prepared a whole fish, which I often serve now at my restaurant in San Francisco. Freshwater crabs are also a mouth-watering specialty of my mother's native region, and as they are prepared in quite a different way in China, I have included further on, two recipes both delicious in their differing ways, which can be used equally well for sea crabs.

Some of my earliest memories are of the festivals which fill the Chinese calendar. Indeed, almost any occasion seemed to be an excuse for a festival or feast. And the most important was the Festival of the New Year, with its symbolism of rebirth and new life. This occurs at the first moon, at the end of January or the beginning of February, according to the lunar calendar. Our calendar sometimes falls far behind, and then an intercalary month is inserted, with the result that there may be two fifth moons in the same year. Each lunar month has its own characteristics, its own weather, flowers, vegetables, and festivals. Accordingly, I have divided this book into twelve moons, as it passes through the seasons of the year and my own life in them.

For at least five days before the Festival of the New Year, the house was alive with preparations. Tsao-chün, the kitchen god, whose picture normally hangs above the stove, had been suitably propitiated, his mouth stuffed with sweetmeats so that he would speak no ill of us when he reported his findings to Yü Huang, the Jade Emperor in heaven; the house had been

8

swept and garnished, and the time for the New Year's Eve feast had arrived.

All stores and even markets were closed for a full week, and it was more than ever necessary to have an ample supply of food in the house. My mother's foresight in pickling and preserving meats, fruits and vegetables now came into its own. Chinese cabbages, crisp and white, were laid away in the cold cellar; watermelons, carefully arranged so that air could circulate between them, lay like bulging vases in neat rows, and large, curiously flat-shaped persimmons were embedded in snow, to be eaten with a spoon, like some exotic sherbet. And great earthenware jars held pickles of all kinds.

As young children we were, as a matter of course, never admitted to the kitchen. That was the domain of the *ta shih-fu*, the head chef, who was inclined to tyrannize over the household, although the majordomo was nominally Lao Li, who had been a family servant for many years. The kitchen was in any case a dangerous place for a child. Razor-sharp cleavers, and hot fires, would be too much of a temptation for young fingers. While the rest of the house hummed with activity, we were being dressed by our wet nurses in fur-lined clothes, embroidered fur hats with earpieces, and quilted embroidered shoes, all homemade. We could always tuck our hands into the opposite sleeves and keep them warm inside the horseshoe cuffs which came down beyond our fingers. I find I still do this to this day whenever the weather is cold, even though I have no cuffs to protect me.

My father always seated himself first and was also served first. We children sat at a separate table until we grew up, and unlike our elders we were not allowed to take morsels from the dish. Each of us was handed food on a very small plate, and had to ask the servant behind our chair, an elder sister or our mother, if we wanted something in particular.

The dishes on this special occasion were well qualified to

offset the cold: a pork shoulder, "red-cooked" in soy and wine to the quintessence of its flavor, of a succulence and aroma to whet the appetite; a whole chicken, baked in clay, to retain all its tenderness and delicacy; and a firepot, typical of northern China, in which all kinds of foods, specially prepared in the same shapes and sizes, are put into a broth. The pot has a central cone through which the heat rises from glowing charcoal underneath, and as the liquid simmers, everyone seated around the table, which is circular, puts his choice of ingredients into the pot. The food looks delicious even before it is cooked, for the chef lays out the plates as an artist composes a picture. Everything possible is round; shrimp balls, all kinds of meat and fish balls—as we say, "round for togetherness." Dried mushrooms, as subtle as truffles, steamed and seasoned, join transparent noodles (*fan-tzu*) and a variety of vegetables to add an infinite range to the aromas rising from the soup. Lotus seeds, steamed with dragon eye and dates, and simmered with dried *kuei-hua* flowers, from the Chinese wild olive, were traditional ingredients of the desserts.

As we drank the steaming broth, or tasted the textures and flavors of meats, mushrooms, the slippery transparency of the noodles contrasted with crisp winter cabbage or lotus root, we could turn our heads from time to time to see through the windows the snowflakes softly falling, which gave an added zest to the feast before us.

Outside, in the darkening lanes, young shop assistants with lanterns were running hither and thither seeking out those who had failed to pay their bills. Everyone was expected to pay his debts before the year's end, just as every shopkeeper expected to claim his due, but after midnight, by custom and tradition, a truce was called. And thus the lanterns continued to dart about, and those who could not, or would not, pay, went into hiding, or were brought guilty and shamefaced into the glow of the lights.

A large fish, cooked whole, glistening with sauce, and lying on its belly as though still swimming, now made its appearance: someone, doubtless, had had to break the ice to get it from the river. Of all the dishes, this was my particular favorite. The fish was first fried a little, then simmered with wine, soy sauce, a hint of garlic, ginger, scallions, and just enough water to make a sauce. The result was a dish of ambrosial delicacy. It also signaled that dinner was coming to an end.

After the feast we would sit up until midnight, watching with sleepy eyes the flickering of tall, splendid candles, *shou-sui*, for at the stroke of twelve we knew we would be one year older (the Chinese, like racehorses, are one year older at the first of the year, whatever the birth date may be). This custom is called *shou-sui* or "watching the year steal away." Firecrackers rent the air, for a happy New Year, or as some believed, to chase away evil spirits, as we were firmly and finally carried off to bed—some of us still awake in anticipation of the excitement of the coming morning.

My father, like all Chinese parents, used to hide money, wrapped up in red paper (*ya-sui ch'ien*) for the children to find on New Year's Day: inside each package, we found he had written a lucky adage and had put in a sprig of evergreen as well, as a good omen. Although our relations with both our parents were extremely formal, without any outward demonstration of affection, my father's advanced views and consideration for others shone through in other ways. None of us was subjected to the binding of the feet, the "lotus feet," as my mother had been, or my father's sister, who took pride in the fact that hers were only three inches long. At the same time, my father always wore the traditional Chinese dress. In winter, over the long robe, he wore a black jacket of satin or cut velvet, as well as a vest trimmed with fur and fur-lined, white or black silk stockings and silk or velvet black shoes with white soles. (In this he was a contrast to my uncle, whom he greatly resembled, Sun Kwei-bo, who, after his return from London, where he became a close friend of Dr. Sun Yat-Sen, always made a point of wearing "foreign" dress. My uncle was also a complete contrast in temperament, rising to the highest position as head of the state railways—he also designed railway coaches—and finally becoming president of the University of Communication. My father took no part in politics, whereas my uncle was one of Dr. Sun Yat-Sen's early revolutionary associates, known as the "old" Kuomintang.)

We all had brand-new clothes for New Year's Day, and the servants, too, were dressed in their best (two tailors were kept constantly at work in the house, making clothes for us, since our dress changed with the seasons). This was the one day in the year when servants were relieved of brushing and sweeping, and had prepared dishes to eat instead of the customary leftovers from our meals. They had to make the most of this one day because Chinese servants did not get vacations, nor was the respite from sweeping altogether out of consideration for them, since the saying was that if you swept on New Year's Day, you swept the gold dust out. We children also gained from traditional customs and superstitions at this time. No one was allowed to punish us or make us cry; and we were permitted to join in the noisy gambling games. Other popular beliefs were that it was unlucky to use a knife or touch scissors; to break anything or let blood; to say anything evil or ill-omened.

The house was gay with red decorations: ornaments of red paper in the shape of Chinese characters, red scrolls brushed with lucky poems hanging from the ceiling beams; and the red camellia, the New Year flower in northern China. To these were added sweet-scented yellow narcissus in bowls filled with colored pebbles; black-stemmed pink flowers, known as *mei-*

hua; heaven bamboo, *t'ien-chu*, red of berry and with bamboo-like leaves; and the flowering plum, filling the air with fragrance, its yellow flowers the color of beeswax. In the south, in Canton, the orange and pomelo are favorites at this season, their golden color symbolizing wealth and good fortune.

Foods especially associated with New Year's Day included *chiao-tzu*, delicate little dumplings fried to a golden brown on one side and stuffed with savory meats, which were considered essential as a beginning. Three or four courses followed, such as hen's eggs poached in chicken soup; thin pancakes, intricately rolled in reverse curves to give them their name, *ju-i*, like the Chinese scepters they resembled, stuffed with eggs and meat; *yüan-hsiao*, tiny marble-sized balls made of glutinous rice, white, or dark and shiny with sugar. *Nien-kao*, rice cakes sometimes filled with date paste or black sesame seeds and flavored with dried *kuei-hua* flowers, were a temptation to youngsters, especially when they were colored with vegetable dyes to look like jade. (In the region of Shanghai, my mother's home, they are usually of a pink color, rich and sweet. There they are sliced, fried lightly, or steamed.) Another kind, *ning-p'u nien-kao*, was sautéed with meat and vegetables, or cooked in a soup. The custom was to eat everything in pairs—two eggs, two *ju-i*, two *yüan-hsiao*, two *nien-kao*—since couples are considered lucky. This also applied to the gifts exchanged at this time: friends and relatives sent servants with tiered lacquer containers in which were canisters of tea, two kinds of preserved fruit, two hams, two chickens; and the boxes could not be sent back empty: twin gifts would weigh them down in return, and red-wrapped money for the servants as well.

Even when we were very young we were expected to kowtow to our parents on this important day, kneeling on the floor and touching our heads to the ground (the name for this ceremonial reverence, *k'o-t'ou*, means "knocking the head"), and all the servants saluted members of the family with the graceful obeisance called *ta-ch'ien*, in which the menservants bent one knee and extended one arm, and the women, with bent knee, modestly laid one arm across the body to the opposite hip. All our servants I remember, as long as we had them, as being loyal, courteous and unbelievably industrious, and at this time of the year there was plenty for them to do—the New Year festivities continued for fifteen days. On the second day, formal calls were paid on relatives and friends, in strict order of precedence: the lower in rank or age calling on the higher or more senior. Like other families of our sort, we kept open house, and tea and delicacies were offered to every caller. Pointed olives were placed on the lid of each teapot, because they looked like *taels*, the Chinese money, and ginkgo nuts were displayed for the same reason. Relatives brought us presents of money, wrapped in red paper, and there were innumerable dinner parties which we attended in our best clothes.

For the first ten days of the festival my sisters and I wore in our hair charming velvet flowers threaded on fine wire, a specialty of Peking, although the exchange of visits continued up to the climax of the celebrations on the fifteenth day, the Feast of Lanterns. Noise, color and flickering lights are forever associated in my mind with that day, when we all set out at twilight with paper lanterns, made in every conceivable shape: a goose, a lotus flower, a carp, a magpie, a phoenix, a lion—painted in brilliant hues; and all the while the rattle of firecrackers roused us to an ever higher pitch of excitement.

After all these festivities, the remaining days of the first moon were something of an anticlimax, although snowflakes still offered the diversion of snowballs and sliding on slippery courtyards, just as the first thaw held out the promise of warmer days. Childhood memories are brief, and it was not long before we were looking forward to the spring.

INTERLUDE

Of Shopping and Its Pleasures

THE PROVISIONING OF A LARGE HOUSEHOLD in Peking necessarily followed a different pattern from that of an American housewife or a European family. Some staple foods had to be bought in bulk, while most other supplies had to be sought out at individual stores; some were bought fresh every day; others were for pickling and storing. The seasons governed all.

Such basic provisions as meat, fish, seafood, vegetables and fruits came within the province of our Number One cook, who used to go to the large market in the quarter where we lived, examining stall after stall in the early morning, to pick out the best quality and the freshest of the provender displayed. He would announce himself as the Number One cook of the Sun family, and the shopkeeper at once came forward to take his orders and haggle over prices. The meats, fish, fruits and vegetables were all protected by awnings and laid out in colorful profusion on stalls, to the noisy music of chaffering and by-play.

Since we were already well known, no payments were made at the time; the shop charged all purchases on credit, and the accounts were settled three times a year: on the Double Fifth, at the August Moon, and just before New Year.

The streets of Peking were alive in the early morning as

long trains of camels from the Gobi Desert wound their way into the city, laden with wood and coal, and the water carriers went from house to house, pulling their heavily burdened carts. Such staple foods as flour and rice were delivered to the back gate in hundred-pound sacks and stacked up in the storage rooms. The sacks came in two-wheeled carts, drawn by mule or donkey; or sometimes a cow was pressed into service. The carter was a familiar figure in the street, always beating the hapless animal drawing the load. When he arrived at the house he hoisted the sacks over his shoulder with a thick rope and staggered through the doorway bent double by the weight. These commodities were charged in the same way as our other provisions.

The street with the finest shops, the Wang Fu Ch'ing Ta Chieh, was the favorite spot for window shopping and most of the stores had British, French or Jewish owners. A big market was in the same locality, across the street from the Grand Hotel. Some fine department stores with imported goods, a famous jewelry store and a few with beautiful Chinese antiques are those I chiefly remember. As children we never bought anything there, as we did not have allowances, although when I was in college I occasionally went there to buy foreign imports.

We sometimes accompanied my mother when she went to the silk and satin store. The proprietor always came up to greet her, bowing, and she would seat herself at the long counter. She was well known there of course, for she was a striking figure, unusually plump and always smiling and amiable. Cigarettes and the best tea or cold soda water and orange juice would be proffered according to the season, and when we were all assuaged, my mother would begin: "What is new today? Not for me, you understand, but something for my daughter."

Some materials would then be presented, to the accompaniment of "What beautiful children you have . . . for which *hsiao-chieh* [daughter]?"

"Today I should like to see something for my Number One daughter."

"Ah, perhaps you would need some of this piping and banding to go with it?"

And to an exchange of comments and compliments, the business of the day would be conducted to a satisfactory conclusion. The yardage was measured with a great display of prestidigitation and a long ruler; and of course my mother had also to choose thread and linings. And the shopkeeper would show flannel, or cotton, according to one's need. Fur was also used for lining in winter. The thread was always sold in various colors in about eighteen-inch skeins, twisted and wound up in rice paper. We never carried parcels: either the chauffeur or a servant fetched them, or they were sent to the house.

The only time money changed hands was at the small shops, which could not be expected to give credit, whereas jewelry, furs and antiques, which were brought to the house by individual merchants, were paid for in cash. Jewelry and furs were wrapped up in cotton squares, *pao-fu*, and tied up inside with silken string; antiques arrived in boxes, with cotton folded around them.

Whole streets were assigned to different goods. Silk, fur, hardware, jade, fans, Peking glass, cloisonné, yarn and thread, leather, velvet flowers—each and every one had its separate location; and as there were many of each to the same street, the owners of the shops had to compete with one another and stock the right merchandise at the right price.

Our servants had to content themselves with buying from the street vendors. Each one had his street cry, offering combs, velvet flowers, lotions or fabrics. Since the domestics were little better than slaves, at our beck and call twenty-four hours a day, seven days a week, with no vacations, they had few opportunities of buying for themselves. My mother sometimes took the very old women servants—never the men—when we went to the park. They did not sit with her, but with us, when we had some refreshments.

Apart from the visits to the yard goods shops, my mother never went shopping unless it were to buy a present or an unusual item at a special store—some choice wines or delicacies that needed to be elaborately wrapped. My father, naturally, never joined these expeditions, although we sometimes accompanied him to the park when he took one of his birds for an airing in a cage, uncovered in summer and in wintertime carefully protected with quilting. We would crowd around to ask what he was eating or drinking—we never dared to sit with him—and with his usual gentle manner he would offer us a sip of his wine or a delicate morsel on the end of a chopstick.

As children we were never allowed to buy from street vendors as our servants did, which made them especially alluring for us. We were told they were dirty and disgraceful. As a result, when I was in high school, I always sneaked out to eat the most basic northern Chinese food at a nearby restaurant, hardly to be dignified by the name, which served a simple *ch'ao-mien* of cabbage and egg, with almost no perceptible vestige of pork, and *kao-t'ang* (free soup) of the most doubtful origin; and *ts'ung-yu ping* ("onion oil cake"). When these cakes were old and hard, the poor often sliced them and added them to a soup made of nothing but bones.

I can hardly exaggerate the effect of the seasons on the way of life in the Peking of my childhood. In the winter our tailor cut out the clothes for the spring; in spring the summer clothes were prepared; in summer our fall and winter wardrobe was made ready, with the assistance of the maidservants, who were kept busy sewing hems and basting seams.

20

Our eating was governed by the same seasonal changes; and unless my mother had some special dainties flown in from the south, we normally ate only those meats and fruits to be found at that time of the year. Our New Year feast was subject to, and traditionally stereotyped by, the provisions available in the winter, or food that could be pickled or preserved by drying or bottling in jars.

To reproduce authentic meals outside China must inevitably present problems, but some measure of success can be achieved if the basic supplies are obtained, either by purchasing them in Chinese shops or ordering them by mail (several sources, with addresses, are given on page 267). The following list, for northern Chinese cooking, is a useful beginning:

five-spice powder	Szechwan peppercorns
fresh ginger root	red bean paste
transparent noodles	cloud ear (sometimes called
dried bean curd	silver ear)
dried bean curd sheets	jujubes (red dates)
sesame seed paste	tiger lily buds ("golden
sesame seed oil	needles")
dried black mushrooms	Chinese sausage
five-star anise	cooking wine (*liao ch'iu*)
bamboo shoots	fresh scallions
small anise	garlic
black wooden ear	dry mustard
soy sauce	"red" Chinese vinegar
hot pepper oil	hot bean sauce

One may need other ingredients from time to time, such as oyster sauce, not normally used in northern cooking; ginkgo nuts, at the time of the August Moon; lichee nuts—rarely found in Peking other than at the New Year; and water chestnuts.

If the reader is already retreating in alarm from this unfamiliar list (which could easily be extended), I can offer assurance that many dishes can be prepared with the use of only one or two of them, as exemplified in the following recipe. Like all those I will give in this book, it is intended to serve from four to six people (but of course much would depend on its placing in a meal—is it to be the main course, or one of several?).

MANDARIN SWEET-SOUR FISH
t'ang-ts'u yü

This is an exquisitely delicate preparation, provided the fish is absolutely fresh and the best materials are used. It might well serve as the main course at a dinner party; in China, since a whole fish is almost invariably one of the last courses at a banquet, it naturally figures in the menu of the New Year's Eve festivities.

1 rock cod, sea bass, carp or
    red snapper, 3 to 3½
    pounds
cornstarch
1 egg (optional)
¼ cup Chinese rice wine or
    dry sherry or water (op-
    tional)
cottonseed oil
garnish: finely sliced carrots
    and celery

SAUCE
¾ cup sugar
½ cup Chinese wine vine-
    gar or a good cider vinegar
½ cup ketchup
½ cup water
juice of 1 lemon
1 teaspoon soy sauce (op-
    tional)
¼ cup cornstarch mixed
    with ¼ cup water

A three-pound fish is the best choice for this dish; at most, it should not weigh more than three and a half pounds. To be sure the fish is straight from the sea, look at the eyes and make sure they are bright and clear and protrude from the head. If they are sunken and clouded over, reject the fish at once. Look also at the gills, and see that they look fresh and pink. Ask the fishmonger to gut the fish and scrape off the scales, but not remove the head and fins, for part of the attraction of serving this dish is that it should look as though it is still swimming.

You can, if you like, prepare the garnish first, although there is plenty of time to do it while the fish is cooking. Slice medium-sized carrots and the whitest possible celery into strips as fine as toothpicks, and refrigerate them, covered, until serving time.

The next stage is to lay the fish on a chopping block, holding the head firmly in a cloth since it is apt to slip, and with a Chinese cleaver make an incision about an inch below the gills, with the blade upright and parallel to the side of the fish. When the skin is penetrated, slice in a semicircular motion, across the width of the fish, with the blade angled slightly inwards. This makes a deep slash to the bone. Repeat the slashing at inch intervals—there will be five or six—down the fish on both sides.

Now hold the fish up by the tail so that the slashes open up like a flower, and sprinkle cornstarch into them and all over the fish. You may, if you wish, substitute a mixture of ¼ cup of cornstarch, the egg, and the Chinese rice wine (or sherry or water) and cover the fish as described, but I think the simple cornstarch method produces a more attractive, fluffier result.

The fish is now ready for deep-frying. Put sufficient cotton-seed oil in your *wok* or fish poacher—the amount will vary with the size of the *wok*, but as a general guide it should reach to within two inches of the top—and heat to 400 degrees. Do not salt or season the fish beforehand as it will make the flesh shrink. When the oil is hot—one should test it with a fat thermometer—put the fish into the oil and cook it for approximately twenty minutes. The time will vary, of course, according to the heat of the oil and the size of the fish. Turn it occasionally, and see that the slashings keep open so that every part is evenly cooked. The fish will emerge a beautiful golden brown from the *wok,* and should be set aside while the sauce is being prepared. Press the fish down a little, to flatten it underneath, so that it will lie upright when it is served.

To make the sauce, combine in a *wok* the sugar, vinegar, ketchup, water, lemon juice, and if you wish to include it, the soy sauce. Make sure you do not use a Japanese wine vinegar —it is too sweet. Bring to a boil over medium heat and simmer for a minute or less, stirring constantly, as the sugar in the mixture introduces the danger of burning. Then stir the carefully blended cornstarch and water into the sauce, and cook until it thickens.

After covering the fish with the glistening, fragrant sauce, arrange the slivers of carrot and celery in a decorative pattern symmetrically along the back on either side. The contrasting colors of orange and greenish-white give a most attractive appearance as the dish is borne into the dining room and displayed to one's guests.

If one wants to try something a little more difficult, a most unusual dish, which figured at our New Year's Eve celebrations, was Beggar's Chicken. It has as great an element of surprise as a Baked Alaska and is almost unknown in this country.

BEGGAR'S CHICKEN
CHIAO-HUA CHI

1 3-pound frying chicken	wine or sherry
1 tablespoon yellow rice	1 heaping teaspoon salt

1 teaspoon sesame seed oil
¼ teaspoon five-spice powder
1 tablespoon soy sauce
1 pound ceramic clay (obtainable in most art supply shops)

STUFFING

¼ cup Virginia ham (the nearest equivalent to Chinese Chin-hua ham)
¼ cup bamboo shoots
¼ cup water chestnuts
¼ cup presoaked black mushrooms

Wash the chicken in the usual way. Do not cut the skin of the chicken anywhere, other than cutting off the tailpiece and trimming off the tips of the wings and the neck opening. Combine the rice wine, salt, sesame seed oil, five-spice powder and soy sauce, and rub the entire bird, inside and out, with the mixture, reserving the residue to add to the stuffing. All the stuffing ingredients should be sliced to the same size— about one inch long and not more than a quarter of an inch wide or thick. After stuffing the bird with them, do not sew it up but re-form it into its natural shape by cradling it in your hands.

Now wrap the bird in a piece of aluminum foil large enough to envelop it completely. Wrap it in the same way in a second square of foil (in China, it was encased in lotus leaves and newspaper). Then insert the chicken into a brown paper bag. Next, mix the ceramic clay to a stiff paste by adding cold water to it gradually, making sure that it is not too watery and is thoroughly mixed. Using a spatula, apply the entire mixture all over the paper bag evenly and smoothly to make a casing about one-quarter of an inch thick.

Preheat the oven for ten minutes at 550 degrees, put in the chicken, and reduce the heat to 475 degrees (the oven must be hot enough or the clay will not set hard). Bake for one hour and three-quarters. Then turn the oven down to about 300 degrees, and bake for thirty minutes more. Remove the bird from the oven and bring it to the table on a metal dish. Strike the clay sharply with a mallet and open. The chicken meat will be so tender and juicy that it can be served with a spoon, and the startling emergence of the chicken from its shell will elicit cries of astonishment from your guests.

SECOND MOON

WHEN THE FIRST SWALLOWS begin to arrive in rows on the gray rooftops of Peking, one knows that spring has come. It is late in arriving in the northern capital, since it officially begins on the fifth day of February, Li Ch'un, or "Beating the Ox," when the first furrow is ceremoniously broken. This ancient ritual was always performed by the Emperor in the grounds of the Forbidden City, watched by the high officials of his court; and the ceremony was then echoed all over the country. Clay figures were made of plowmen and oxen, which were broken up and carried away for good luck, and all kinds of prognostications were made from the colors and shapes of the pieces. I must admit, as a girl brought up to city life, I never saw the ceremony, and the change of season was signaled for me by the swallows and the first hint of thaw. All through the winter the window ledges of our Peking house had been covered with thick yellow dust, borne on the fierce wind from the Gobi Desert, but now the gusts were dying down, and with breath-taking suddenness, the black branches of the ying-ch'un hua, the "welcome spring" winter jasmine opened their fragrant yellow flowers, the harbinger of warmer days. More and more birds filled the sky, and when the swallows began to nest in the eaves of one's house, it was a good omen.

The twelfth day of the second moon was the Festival of Flowers. The tree peonies in their raised beds received particularly loving attention from my father, for they are the symbol of spring; and around the wide, seat-like rims he also placed small *bonsai*, which had been kept until now in a heated greenhouse; and in due time the cherry blossom and pear came to augment the drifts of color.

On the far side of the main courtyard was the principal reception room, occupying the whole width of one side of the court and laid out in rigid and uncomfortable symmetry. Opposite the entrance, against the far wall, was an altar on which was set out a group of ritual vases, an incense burner and a jade screen. All the furniture was of teak and arranged in pairs; and the straight-backed chairs, elaborately carved, offered no comfort to the sitter, who, in any event, could not lean back as that was considered impolite. Fortunately, what were considered more modern rooms, with cushioned and padded furniture, adjoined, separated from the vast main hall by openwork screens. The bright colors of silks and porcelains and the more subdued tones of painted scrolls looked well against the ivory-white walls and black woodwork.

We never spent a night away from our own houses, so that I never knew what it was to stay for any length of time with friends and relations, although our cousins, the children of my father's brother, Sun Kwei-bo, came to live with us after their mother died of cancer. My uncle then remarried, scandalizing my parents by choosing a very beautiful young woman from the Pa-ta Hu-t'ung, or "Flowery Quarter," who had no interest in the children. My mother felt that no good would come of the match, and events proved her right. My uncle spent a fortune on his young wife, and when he died, many valuables were found to be missing.

My room, like my sisters', was almost at the back of the rows of single-storied buildings and courtyards which made up our rambling house. Our rooms adjoined the quarters of the women servants so that we could have help within easy

30

reach; and each was provided with a storeroom for clothes. The straight Chinese clothes were folded in three, with the sleeves behind, and laid away in trunks of soft leather at the end of each season. Winter furs were also stored, with mothballs, and received special attention in May or early June, during the damp, hot season, when they were taken out and shaken, away from the sunlight, and brushed along the lie of the fur with brushes of natural bristle, before being folded in rice paper and put away again until the winter.

The last row of buildings, housing the women's quarters, kitchen and storerooms, also had an entrance, much smaller than the main gateway on the other side of the house, which opened into the street behind, and we sometimes used this when coming back from school. A small guardroom, with a manservant, kept watch over it, and it was through this door that supplies for the household were delivered.

We rarely went to our country home in the winter because there were no roads as such, and after the first thaw trails became quagmires. When we went at other seasons we always enjoyed the freedom and informality of the life there. It was a joy for a small child to be released in the open spaces, to play among the flowers, hide among the fruit trees, or throw millet to the noisy chorus of ducks and hens. Sometimes we helped, as we thought, to pick beans or cucumbers, or came across a scarlet patch of wild strawberries, hidden close to the ground. But now there was mud everywhere, and carts drawn by cows were the sole means of transport, unless one was carried on a servant's back, which indeed is one of my first recollections of Ch'ang-hsin Tien, where our country place was, and the manner in which I was first taken to school.

My brothers had been educated by tutors, and my sisters by the Sisters of the Sacred Heart, but I went to the P'ei-man, the fashionable American missionary school known as the Bridgeman Academy, in the same eastern quarter of the city where we lived, and where, incidentally, all the best schools were located.

We were awakened at half-past six, dressed, assisted by our *amahs*, in our school uniform, which was a royal-blue smock under which, in winter, we could wear anything we liked as long as the uniform covered everything. After the usual preliminaries of washing our faces and brushing our teeth, we youngsters sat down at the same round table for breakfast, *tsao-fan*, or "early rice," at which the basic food was a bowl of hot congee, or *chou*. In the north, this is prepared very plainly of rice and water boiled without salt to form a thin gruel. Four dishes are usually served to eat with the congee, which acts as a neutral background, not unlike Scotch porridge. Holding the bowl in the left hand, we selected a morsel of lightly pickled cucumber, or a thinly cut sliver of sweet-tasting turnip, dipped the morsel in the congee with our chopsticks, and ate. The other dishes were often fresh bean curd, bland and mild, seasoned with soy sauce; thousand-year eggs, especially well prepared in Peking—the whites have concentric rings of a beautiful amber brown, the yolks are dark gray—and they are sliced in half lengthwise to reveal the markings, like some rare agate; and shrimp, sprinkled with soy sauce after being rapidly cooked in hot, slightly salted water until they turned pink. When we had visitors, six or eight choices would be set out—an elaborate breakfast to honor the visiting relations. For additional delicacies, the kitchen might serve up fried minced pork, cooked until it became a deliciously savory, reddish-brown crumble; crisp bamboo shoots, lightly marinated, with chewy mushrooms; and fermented bean curd, which has something of the taste and consistency of Camembert cheese. The simple, unflavored congee, unaccompanied by anything rich or fatty, is typical of northern Chinese tastes. In the south, in Canton, the preference is for much richer breakfasts. The congee has salt and sugar added, as well as Chinese parsley (coriander); and to dip into it are such foods as slices of fresh ginger root, pieces of young squid, Chinese greens, and even slices of raw fish, which are partially cooked by dipping them into the boiling hot gruel; and a raw egg is sometimes added for extra richness.

Differences between northern breakfast habits and those of other regions are affected largely by mealtime customs. For instance, in parts of the coastal areas and more inland, in Hunan, it is usual to have three meals a day, all very similar, served with dry, boiled rice, accompanied by varied dishes. In the south and west, the two-meal system is the rule, and one eats in the morning and the afternoon. This is not as austere as it sounds, for in Canton three light meals are often dovetailed in between: a light breakfast is followed by a solid meal before noon; then an assortment of *tien-hsin*, or "touch-the-heart," is eaten at midday, with tea; dinner, served late in the afternoon, is similar to the morning meal; and finally, a collation of seasoned congee at midnight rounds off the day.

Further complications can be added by religious restrictions. Orthodox Buddhists eat only vegetables on the first and fifteenth of each month (my mother still observed this custom, as well as forgoing meat altogether during June, when there is also an embargo on wine and one may eat only cold dishes); and Buddhist monks eat no meat at all. In Mongolia, beef and lamb are favorite meats. The Mohammedans, concentrated mainly in Kansu and Chinghai, eschew pork as unclean, which is otherwise the principal and favorite meat of the Chinese. In spite of the Buddhist rule regarding vegetables, the Chinese cooks have discovered many ingenious ways of alleviating the monotony of vegetarianism; whole banquets are devised at which the dishes bear all the appearance of rare meats, fowl and even fish, even though they stemmed originally from the vegetable garden. Much ingenuity is expended in creating these dishes, in which bean curd (*tou-fu*) plays a large part. Thus the word of Buddha is observed to the letter, if not in the spirit.

All this, however, did not worry us as we hurried through our meal. To the boys in the family, and there was one quite close in age to me, was granted the special privilege of a crispy bun, or *ping*, shiny-brown outside and filled with soft strips of steamed dough, much like the *shao-ping* we ate wrapped around pieces of savory Mongolian lamb at dinner. We also ate, and I particularly liked, the long strips of *yu-t'iao* bread, fried to a warm brown, which could be dipped in our hot goat's milk, or in the white bean milk we drank as an alternative.

I was now past the age of being carried to school by my *amah*, and breakfast over, we climbed in, two to a rickshaw, and sped away to school. We learned the classics, poems, writing and painting, singing and intricate paper cutting; and at half-past twelve we rode home in a rickshaw again for lunch, for which one hour was allowed. School continued in the afternoon until five o'clock, by which time, in winter, it was already dark. Looking back, it seems a long day for a small child, but I do not remember complaining of it at the time. Embroidery did not enter the curriculum until high school, a subject begun with flowers on a pillowcase, and progressing to embroidered tablecloths and handkerchiefs on fine Shantung linen.

If we felt especially hungry while at school and a free period gave us the opportunity, we would hurry to a street vendor or small restaurant and buy an onion cake, *ts'ung-yu ping*, fried and flavorsome, and eat it with the cheapest of all soups, made from leftovers, ominously named "Wash-the-Pot." Having no allowances and few funds other than what we had been given at the New Year, we were chronically short of money.

In our free time we were endlessly resourceful, unlike children today, making our own shuttlecocks from two *cash* tied together. These coins have a square central opening, through which we put goose quills, cut to about a quarter of an inch in length; these in turn were stuffed with carefully trimmed chicken feathers. We then had the wherewithal for a competitive game, kicking the shuttlecock up in the air first with one heel and then the other, and seeing who could keep it up longest. We had many elaborate ways of bouncing balls, and with skipping and handball as well, we had no lack of amusement. Gymnastics came later, in high school, performed in the open air since there was no gymnasium. We also played basketball, tennis, Ping-Pong and volleyball—and in winter, badminton at the YWCA. I was considered rather a tomboy, liking all kinds of sports.

The lake in Pei Hai Park was a perennial attraction, for the beautiful expanse, with its graceful bridges, undulating shoreline, water lilies and lotus flowers, also had rowboats, and in the winter offered the possibility of ice skating.

When our school day ended, we began to think of dinner, which was prepared at half-past six, and as usual, my father was seated first, sipping an aperitif in leisurely fashion. We children sat down at about seven o'clock, and were handed portions on very diminutive plates. We learned to eat tidily, our right hand holding the chopsticks. Lefthanded children received short shrift in China as being unlucky, and I would have been rapped sharply over the knuckles had I so misused my chopsticks or soup spoon. Neatness in eating had other virtues since dry cleaning did not exist in those days; at most, spots could be removed if the cloth was not too deeply stained, and we took care therefore not to spill any food or leave a grain of rice; and all this had to be achieved without a table napkin: a hot towel at the end of the meal was our only recourse for a moment of carelessness.

After some time for play came the hour for bed. As I grew older, I loved to read at night, novels, and especially modern novels, and would boast at school how much I had read the night before. Ten o'clock was by then the time to put out the lights, but I would wheedle my *amah* into letting me stay up longer, and she was usually complaisant. Our wet nurses really spoiled us, giving in to us to excess; and my third sister's *amah* was so jealously possessive that she told my sister she was her real mother, and attempted to alienate her completely from our natural parents: she stayed on with my sister for years. My fifth sister had her *amah* with her until she died in her service. In spite of this, I can recall no problems that I needed to have resolved, only a happy existence, except when fights broke out between my younger brother, my younger sister and me. My mother and all the servants, to our constant chagrin, were always on the side of the sons of the family when it came to a fracas.

Since school times and classes were uniform, as soon as school ended for the day the boys hurried to see the girls emerge. It was not easy to get acquainted because it was out of the question to whistle or strike up a conversation. Usually a boy had a sister at the school who effected an introduction. In this way my elder brother, Sun Shiu-chi, came to know Wu Chuan-juen, a tall, very beautiful girl with long legs and a quick temper. She was hopelessly spoiled and led my brother an endless dance, for he was infatuated with her. My brother felt that he had completely lost a weekend if he did not see her, and to my mother's consternation, stayed in his room and refused to come to meals. My mother, or sometimes one of my elder sisters, had to buy presents for him to give her, as young men in China were shy of shopping for gifts for their girl friends.

Eventually my brother became officially engaged, but Chuan-juen's mother kept insisting that she wanted to keep her longer at home, so that the marriage did not take place until my brother was about thirty years of age and had been engaged for seven years. It was not exactly a convenient marriage for us: although she came of a very wealthy family, and therefore brought a handsome dowry of clothes and jewels into our house, she made all the servants wait on her, and even kept my parents waiting at mealtimes. This, of course, was an appalling solecism in old China, where everyone of adult age ate at the same hour and elders were treated with a proper deference.

My younger brother, Sun Jun-chi, married some years later, in 1947 or 1948. His choice, Chang Hua-yi, was hardly more acceptable to my parents as she was the daughter of a Manchu warlord. My brother was then working for the government, in the air force; her sisters had married air force pilots, and she and my brother had met by this route. Hua-yi's father took to my brother instantly at their first meeting, told his daughter she would be lucky if she married him, and gave him a magnificent gold watch and chain. My parents showed less enthusiasm; and as it turned out, she, like her father, had a terrible temper. Since in the China of those days the saying was "four generations under one roof," and the harmony of a united family was a cherished concept, the two daughters-in-law were distinctly out of key. Nevertheless, to have a son married is to gain grandchildren, and my elder brother had two boys and a daughter, and the younger, one son. During pregnancy my sisters-in-law were expected to wear bright colors and change their clothes every day, to ensure good fortune for the offspring. If I sound a little uncharitable about these two girls, I will also allow that living in one's inlaws' house was quite a difficult prospect for a new wife in China: the only person she would know at all among the crowd of strange faces was her husband.

Towards the end of the second moon, in March, came the time of Ch'ing Ming, corresponding to the Christian Easter, the Festival of Sweeping the Tombs, not at all a sad occasion, but rather a time of rejoicing, as one made beautiful the tombs of one's ancestors, and offered them their favorite food, wine and flowers. Thirty days were set aside for these rites, of which the first was thought the most auspicious. Ordinarily, there was a custodian of the tombs, who profited considerably from the festivities since he usually ended up by eating all the good things. The second moon was also a time for enjoying the spring flowers and picnicking; and no incongruity was felt in paying respect to departed relatives at the same moment as one was enjoying the manifestations of new life in flowers and foliage, or eating *al fresco:* death and rebirth went hand in hand. All the same it would simply not have occurred to my parents or to my father's brother, to take us out for a rural excursion: we had *amahs* and servants to look after us, and it was not the custom.

My father's two brothers-in-law were both military officers of high rank; his elder sister had married General Shueh Shang-wu, and his younger sister, General Ting Gin, the senior ranking officer in the air force. General Gin's home, as I recall, was full of airplane models. He had been the first to sign up, at the age of seventy, to fight the Japanese and was bitterly disappointed to be rejected on the grounds of age. My sister Sun Chin and I were to stay with him in Chungking years later. Both these uncles were remote and dignified figures who might visit us, and whom we might visit in return, but for the young it was a purely formal and ceremonious relationship. Our parents certainly loved us, but they never kissed us or showed any emotion, and their days followed a different course. My mother was always at her embroidery or playing *mah jong* or supervising all the multifarious activities of the kitchen. My father was always tending to the plants or peering at his stamp collection through a magnifying glass; together they would go to the classic Chinese opera. They also had a partiality for motion pictures, where we met on common ground: we could attend free since the family owned a number of cinemas in Peking and Tientsin. My parents always took a siesta in the afternoon, and afterwards drank tea, with *wonton* or something sweet. We also had a siesta, but only in the summertime, during the extreme heat. The bedding was then protected by very finely woven straw, in delicate patterns, even to the pillowcases, and all the pieces of furniture were covered with it—straw was much cooler to sit on, as well as for sleeping, or the afternoon nap.

My own recollection of picnics is of little expeditions by bus, shepherded by a school mistress, to the Summer Palace or the Western Hills, taking our food, cold, save for a thermos flask of tea, wrapped in a square of silk. This was first tied, one corner diagonally to another, and then a second time with the remaining diagonals, corner to corner. According to the size of the square, one could put one's wrist through the top fold, or slip it over one's shoulder, just as I have seen Japanese women in Tokyo carrying their shopping to this day. When we had settled in some attractive spot, we enjoyed peering into each other's packages and exchanging tidbits with our particular school friends; their supplies always seemed more exciting than ours, or had the charm of novelty. I cannot conceive of our parents or relations taking us for picnics: the gap between the generations was unbridgeable, far wider, I believe, than is the case in America today; and I do not believe, as is often alleged, that it was owing solely to respect for one's elders: in my experience, the feelings Chinese children of my time had for their parents was closer to fear, or as one might more truly say, fear of the unknown.

INTERLUDE

Of the Unexpected Guest
and the Resourceful Hostess

WHEN WE SAT DOWN TO MEALS AS A FAMILY, we adopted a much simpler mode of eating than prevailed at the New Year Festival, when guests were entertained. Such meals are known as *pien-fan*, "casual rice," or what might be termed home cooking. All the dishes were brought to the table at once, centering around a bowl of soup, which provided the beverage for the repast.

If we had any unexpected visitors, usually cousins, aunts, or elder married sisters, who might have dropped in to play *mah jong*, they would be invited to stay to dinner as a matter of course. This produced an exchange of formal demurs and renewed solicitations. When my mother first invited a guest to remain, she would immediately reply, "Oh, please, do not go to a lot of trouble, I really cannot inconvenience you." And my mother, in return, would answer, "It is no more than a little casual dinner, just 'four dishes and one soup.'" This last phrase is a conventional expression, *szu-t'sai yi-t'ang*, literally translated, and in truth my mother would already have made a mental note to instruct our cooks to add some extra dishes from our resourceful larder of stored foods.

In general, the family meal included a meat dish, of which a favorite in our household during the colder months was *hung-shao jou*, red-cooked pork. The pork required long cooking in soy sauce, since the pork in China is fresh and tougher than the pork sold in America. In this slow stewing method the meat, although it loses in bulk, gains immeasurably in flavor.

Fish would provide another dish, and it was sometimes what we knew as *tou-pan la-yü,* that is, "hot spicy bean sauce fish," cooked whole. Such crustaceans as shrimp were extremely expensive, and would not appear on simple occasions; crab was seasonal, and lobster almost unknown in the north.

A bean curd plate, in one of its many forms, would almost certainly be included, such as fresh *tou-fu* and green scallions, the scallions imparting some of their flavor to the bean curd, which in itself has little or none, but providing a delicate contrast of texture, a soft sliding companion for the crisp scallions, rapidly stir-fried together in the *wok.*

For a vegetable dish,—we distinguish bean curd as a separate category—we often would eat *pai-ts'ai ch'ao tung-ku,* Chinese cabbage with black mushrooms, another congenial meeting of taste and tactile variety, and elusive fragrance. A variation would be to serve *p'ao-ts'ai,* vegetables pickled in the Szechwanese way, with rice, which can be hot on the tongue.

For the soup, a typical kind was *fan-tzu t'ang,* "transparent-noodle soup," with a chicken broth base and vegetables, light and nourishing at the same time.

Faced with the problem of extra chopsticks—another conventional expression on the part of the hostess was that an extra person at table required no more inconvenience than placing a pair of *k'uai-tzu* (chopsticks) on it—my mother could easily call upon "thousand-year" eggs, pickled in lime for some six weeks, which made a delicious, smooth beginning. Chinese sausage, steamed with Chinese bacon, was an alternative, since my mother made her own sausages, from pure pork meat and pork fat. These were kept in skins made from the intestines of lambs, which were just the right size. Eggs were a great standby in family cooking, either hard-boiled, red-cooked with pork, or freshly steamed with dried shrimp and a little ham; or in the form of *ts'ung-ch'ao chi-tan*, green onions with chicken eggs. Eggs with Chinese chives, stronger in flavor than the Western herb, was another favorite.

None of the dishes I have described is difficult to prepare. Their simplicity of execution was the reason they could all make their appearance at the same time. To present six or seven elaborate dishes simultaneously would tax the skill of any cook, especially as the actual cooking time of many *chefs d'oeuvre* of *ch'ao* (stir-fry cooking) is often measured in split-second decisions between minute and minute, preceded by hours of careful preparation.

The Western hostess, under no compulsion to serve six or seven dishes, may compose a dinner as follows, selected from those I have described. The starred dishes are possible additions.

MENU FOR THE UNEXPECTED GUEST
Steamed Eggs
Red-cooked Pork Shoulder
*Transparent Noodle Soup
Black Mushrooms with Chinese Cabbage
*Spicy Hot Fish
*Bean Curd and Green Scallions
Fresh Fruit in Season: Persimmons, Apples, Pears

STEAMED EGGS
CH'UN CHI-TAN

This is a delicious dish, simplicity itself, which can be swiftly made for lunch or dinner; it resembles a cloud-light custard.

Its speed in making is an advantage, as the dish that follows it needs to be set in motion two hours earlier.

2 eggs
2 cups cold water
1 dozen peeled and
    deveined raw shrimp
3 or 4 Chinese dried
    shrimp for extra zest
    (optional)

1 tablespoon finely chopped
    scallions
pinch of salt
garnish: chopped fresh cori-
    ander

Crack the eggs into a small mixing bowl and beat lightly with bamboo chopsticks or a wire beater. Add the water, shrimp, scallions and salt, and mix until blended. Have a Chinese bamboo steamer (or a double boiler) ready, heated. Place the bowl in the steamer, cover, and steam for a scant fifteen minutes.

RED-COOKED PORK SHOULDER
HUNG-SHAO T'I-P'AN

In most meat dishes, particularly those *ch'ao*-cooked (stir-fried), the meat is sliced or diced before cooking so that the pieces are not only small enough to be picked up easily in one's chopsticks without further cutting, but also cook quickly and evenly. In this recipe the pork is cooked whole and carved later. Red-cooking refers to the use of soy sauce, which imparts the characteristic deep red color to the meat. In a Chinese kitchen the meat would be prepared in a *wok*, a kind of cast-iron pot with a lid, but a Dutch oven or any cooking pot that distributes the heat evenly will be satisfactory.

1 4-pound pork butt or
    shoulder with the skin

left on
2 cups water

1 cup soy sauce

2 finely sliced pieces of
    fresh ginger root 2½
    inches long, or 2 cloves
    of garlic if preferred

3 or 4 cloves of five-star
    anise

1 tablespoon Chinese
    cooking wine or dry
    sherry

½ cup sugar (scant)

First, scald the pork by plunging it into boiling water. When the water comes again to a boil, remove the meat, rinse it thoroughly in cold water, and put it into a *wok*. Combine the water and all the other ingredients (except the sugar and wine) and pour the mixture over the pork. Bring to a boil, reduce the heat to a simmer, and cover. Cook until tender (approximately one and a half hours), turning the meat from time to time. Remove the lid, add the sugar and wine, and increase the heat to reduce the sauce. Baste the meat until the liquid is reduced to one cupful. This should take about fifteen minutes. You must take care that the sugar, which helps to make a beautiful glaze over the red color of the meat, does not burn and ruin both appearance and taste. The wine is also introduced late because prolonged cooking of wine makes the taste bitter. Finally, test the meat with a long wooden kitchen chopstick or skewer, which will enter the meat easily when it is done. Slice the meat, cover with the sauce, and serve immediately.

The meat reduces considerably in the cooking, so that it would be sufficient for four to six servings in a Chinese dinner with several main dishes. The pork, cooked in this way, is equally good when cold. It is then sliced and eaten with a steamed bun (*ping*), sandwich fashion.

BLACK MUSHROOMS WITH CHINESE CABBAGE

PAI-TS'AI CH'AO TUNG-KU

This dish can be made equally well with spinach or Chinese chard, and is rapidly *ch'ao*-cooked (stir-fried).

5–6 ounces dried, thick black mushrooms

1½ pounds Chinese cabbage

vegetable oil

1 teaspoon salt

1 cup chicken stock (see page 49)

2 cups fresh bean sprouts (optional)

2 cups cooked transparent noodles (optional)

a few drops sesame seed oil

To prepare the mushrooms, soak them in lukewarm water for about two hours, then squeeze them dry. Soak them once more in fresh lukewarm water, this time overnight. When ready to use them, drain, and then cut each mushroom in half. You should have 2 to 3 cups of mushroom halves for this recipe. (Two kinds of mushrooms are sold in dried form in Chinese groceries, the thin and the thick. The thin are good for shredded use, while the thick provide larger pieces and are therefore preferred for this dish.)

To prepare the Chinese cabbage, cut the stems in 1-inch squares and tear the leaves into pieces to match in volume. You need 2 to 3 cups of each. Keep them in cold water until ready to use; then drain and add.

Heat the vegetable oil in a *wok*, coating the sides thoroughly, and then pour off all but the bare minimum. Add the mushroom halves, the drained cabbage stems and leaves, and the salt. Stir-cook for thirty seconds, then add the chicken stock and toss-stir for another thirty seconds. Cover the *wok*, cook for thirty seconds longer, then ladle out all but a quarter of a cup of the liquid. Continue to stir-cook until the vegetables are done—a matter of moments. If you wish to add the bean sprouts or the transparent noodles, now is the time to do so. Then add the sesame seed oil to give the dish a shining brilliance.

In northern China, Chinese cabbage, while grown and harvested only in the autumn months, was available all the year round by being stored in a cool, dark place in aerated stacks. I remember clearly how much sweeter it tasted if there was a frost before it was picked.

TRANSPARENT NOODLE SOUP
FAN-TZU T'ANG

This is a most adaptable soup, of which the first essential is a good chicken stock.

4 cups chicken stock (see below)

¼ pound transparent noodles

½ pound Chinese cabbage leaves or spinach

1 ounce dried shrimp or a few slices Virginia ham

⅓ teaspoon salt

CHICKEN STOCK

1 good fat hen, 3½ to 4 pounds

pig bones, cracked

¼ pound Virginia ham

2 large chunks fresh ginger root, 3 inches long, pounded

2 large whole scallions

To prepare the chicken stock, wash and prepare the chicken, put it in a large pot, and cover with cold water. Add the pig bones and the ham, and bring to a boil over high heat, uncovered. Remove the scum from the top until the stock is clear. Then add the ginger and scallions. At this point, if necessary, add more boiling water to keep the chicken completely submerged. Cover and simmer for about two hours. By that time all the goodness will be in the stock, which can

49

then be refrigerated and used as desired after removing any fat that has risen to the top and reheating to the boil.

To prepare the soup, first soak the noodles in hot water until they soften, then drain. Pour the stock into a pot and add the shrimp first: they play an important role in awakening the flavors and therefore have priority. Next, put in the noodles, and lastly the cabbage leaves (if spinach is used instead it must be well washed to remove any grit), which need only about five minutes of cooking. If Virginia ham is used instead of shrimp, it should be added last or its flavor will be cooked away. Finally, add the salt. The timing will vary slightly according to the vegetable used, so that you must exercise your judgment in assessing the moment of perfection.

FISH WITH HOT SPICY BEAN CURD SAUCE
TOU-PAN LA-YÜ

This dish is admirably suited to warm a cold guest on a winter's evening, and is characteristic of the Szechwan style, which has a predilection for pepper and spice.

1 whole fresh fish, under
   3 pounds
cornstarch
1½ cups chicken stock
   (see page 49)
cottonseed or peanut oil

SAUCE
1 teaspoon shredded
   ginger root
1 tablespoon Szechwan
   hot bean curd paste

1 teaspoon Szechwan
   pepper
2 tablespoons soy sauce
dash of Chinese cooking
   wine
1 tablespoon thick black
   mushrooms, presoaked
   and diced (see page 48)
2–3 ounces finely sliced
   lean pork
2 or 3 shredded fresh
   scallions

The fish, which may be fresh rock cod, sea bass, or a fresh-water fish such as carp (which is, however, extremely bony), or whatever is locally available, must be absolutely fresh, as I have described in the recipe for Mandarin sweet sour fish, and it must be prepared in the same way: slashed and powdered with cornstarch all over (see page 22). If you cannot get a whole fresh fish of the right size, the center cut or tail of a larger fish will prove equally good, or almost so, although it will not look quite as decorative on the table. Be very careful, of course, not to break the fish gall or its bitterness will ruin the dish before you have begun.

Instead of deep-frying the fish, put enough oil in the *wok* to brown the fish lightly on both sides, over high heat. Throw out the oil, after taking out the fish, and lower the heat to a simmer. Put the fish back in the *wok* with the chicken stock, cover, and simmer for twenty minutes. Mix all the sauce ingredients together and stir-fry lightly in an oiled *wok*. Then pour the sauce over the fish and simmer for another fifteen minutes, turning the fish occasionally to ensure that the flavors penetrate deeply into it. Nice judgment must be exercised about the final timing: when the sauce begins to dry out a little, the fish is adjudged done.

Rush the spicy hot fish to the table and eat, as I did as a child, in silence, to avoid swallowing any bones. Your guest will not fail to signify his appreciation afterwards.

BEAN CURD AND GREEN SCALLIONS
CH'ING-TS'UNG CH'AO TOU-FU

The classic simplicity of this dish may lull one into thinking that it is easy to prepare. Nevertheless, beware the fragility of the bean curd, and the speed at which the ingredients are cooked. Chinese simplicity is often the height of sophistication.

4 pieces fresh bean curd	1 tablespoon oyster sauce
vegetable oil	pinch of salt
2 long green scallions	pinch of sugar

Cut the bean curd into one-inch squares, half an inch thick. Cut the scallions, including the green part, into inch-long pieces. In a *wok*, heat a little cottonseed oil to the sizzling point over high heat and add the bean curd; stir-fry until brown. Then add the scallions, oyster sauce, soy sauce and salt, and rapidly stir-fry until the sauce begins to reduce or dry out a little (about one minute). Add the sugar at the last moment; it both provides a glaze and heightens the flavor, which is by now fully imparted to the bland bean curd. Do not add the sugar earlier on; it burns easily and will spoil the dish.

"STEEPED" VEGETABLES
P'AO TS'AI

Pickled vegetables are so universally popular in Szechwan as an accompaniment to meals that a little saucer for them makes a regular appearance on every restaurant table in Chungking or Chengtu. The pickles are prepared with extreme care and the earthenware jars in which they are stored are always kept meticulously clean. When pickles are taken out of a jar, a special new pair of long chopsticks extracts the pieces.

Any crisp, textured vegetable can be used, cut into *t'iao,* or "stalks," uniform in size and shape. Each should be about one and a half inches long and about pencil-thick. The following reproduces faithfully the method of preparation in Szechwan, although it would naturally differ, in the smaller details, from one family to another:

long string beans
Chinese turnip
Chinese cabbage
Chinese cucumbers
small carrots
red peppers

Szechwan peppercorns
4 quarts water
¼ cup salt
½ cup *kaoliang* or *Mao-t'ai*
      wine

First wash all the vegetables thoroughly in fresh, cold water
and dry them. Then cut them into strips as described above;
all the strips must be of this exact size. The one exception is
the cabbage, which is cut into two-inch squares.

Heat the water to the boiling point and add the salt; then
pour it into a fresh bowl and allow it to cool. When the liquid
is lukewarm, add the wine (which prevents fermentation).

Now put the cabbage and vegetables into a jar with the
cooled fluid, seal it tightly, and leave it for five days. The
Szechwan jar used for this purpose has an extra flange,
forming a second neck, which makes a channel around the
inside of the top of the jar. The lid is placed over the top of
this second neck, which is slightly below the outside one, and
the space is filled with more water, completely sealing off the
lid, and kept topped up. The liquid in which the pickles are
steeped can always be used after reboiling. Preserved in this
way, the vegetables retain their crispness and color.

DESSERT

Fresh fruit was a favorite in my childhood. It was served at
the end of a meal and varied according to the season. In
winter we most frequently had persimmons, apples, or pears.
Alternatively, we might have Peking preserved fruits, including apricots and red dates, accompanied by dry Chinese pastries; but never, in any circumstances, almond or fortune
cookies.

THIRD MOON

Spring is short in the northern capital, a prized interval between winter and summer, and in April the spring flowers have their brief moment of perfection. In Pei Hai Park, displays of peonies drew many people, attracted by the blooms of such rarities as the black and green varieties, opening in the early warmth. More and more folk were to be seen standing in the streets or collected at a corner, their arms akimbo, enjoying the sunshine; and in every courtyard of our house, as the sun rose higher in the sky and the shadows shortened, the dogs yawned and went to sleep on the warm stones; and our multi-colored cats stretched, tested their claws on the wooden uprights of the verandas, and began a fastidious toilette.

Our lives continued their quiet ways, within the close confines of the family circle. The family was indeed so all-embracing and all-pervading that I think it needs a little explanation. No Chinese is in any doubt of his exact relationship to any member of his family, however remote, since a word exists for each degree of kinship: the addition of the qualifying syllables to a name on being introduced, say, to some distant cousin by adoption, immediately reveals the precise family connection. In our own large family, our parents called us by our own names or by nicknames; and as my Number Four and Five sisters were twins, they were always referred to as Big Sister and the Little One; and I was always known as Number Seven.

What few members of my mother's family still lived, were in the south, in Shanghai or Wu-hsi, but all my father's relatives dwelt, as we did, in T'ung Chen, in the east quarter of the city near the Imperial Palace, and were therefore continually exchanging calls with us. It was seldom indeed that any strangers came to the house, unless it were a close friend of a relation, and I can recall only two cousins near enough in age for me to play with, as the generations did not mix. We were on perfectly good terms with our elder sisters within narrow limits, but as they were, in some instances, ten to twenty years older, they did not talk to us; and in such a large group of buildings, spread out on one level, we did not see them often. Even at mealtimes we had no common ground: we were not supposed to join in any conversation, and one certainly never sat down with one's elders to discuss anything. I do not think I loved my sisters in early childhood; because they were so much senior, we did not even fight, that convenient safety valve even in the best families. I feared them more like parents, and when they scolded us, on the rare occasions when they did speak, we accepted the reproof, assuming they knew better, from their weight of years and experience. It was a correct but not warm relationship, and I did not really come to know my sisters with affection until after I was married.

When my elder sisters went to visit the elder daughters of my uncle, General Ting Gin, and took me along, I would play with the youngest. My sisters would talk about embroidery, sewing, poems, or cooking: we would have our childish games quite separately. The gap in understanding was complete, and as a result, my schoolmates were always much closer to me than members of my own family. For one thing, school was completely apart; my parents never came to it or talked to the teachers; and in the rare instances when the school had to complain of a child's behavior, the matter would normally be settled by an exchange of letters. We were, on the whole, remarkably well behaved.

In spite of the narrow range of playmates, I remember this period as a happy time, and the spring, after all, brought a two-week vacation, during which the school arranged picnics. Spring also brought its seasonal foods, such as *mu-shi* pork, consumed with a *pao-ping* or a *ch'un-ping* (spring bun). Fresh beans had their hour, and sliced pork with *chiu-ts'ai* (green chives), or the yellow kind, *chiu-huang*, blanched by being grown under cover. We would eat *shao-ping* with five-spiced pork, in an inspired version of the sandwich, or Chin-hua ham, sliced and shredded and wrapped up in the bun, or cucumber, our delicate-skinned, seedless Chinese kind, or shredded chicken—the possibilities were many. At lunch, a dish of noodles with hot pickled vegetables contrasted the softness of the one with the crisp chewiness of the others. These dishes were for the family circle: if relatives came in any number, or we were entertaining several families at one time, it was the opportunity for *ch'un-yen*, a spring feast. Often my parents and my uncles took turns in entertaining in this way; but if one was going to be host to a large number, it was customary for my family, and those like them, to arrange to have four round tables, eight or ten to a table, at a good restaurant, or alternatively, have a famous chef come from one of the best restaurants to prepare the banquet at home.

The *ta shih-fu* would arrive at midday, with an assistant, to set everything in motion, and all the food was brought from his establishment in enormous bamboo trays, one on top of the other, borne on the end of long bamboo poles slung over the shoulders of coolies who might have had to carry these heavy burdens for several miles.

59

The master chef did not do any of the preliminary work, but gave orders how he wished the various meats, fowl, game, fish, vegetables, or any other materials, to be chopped, sliced, minced, marinated, or whatever else was needed in advance, and only at the last would he demonstrate his art in the actual cooking. He even brought his own cooking stoves, like large oil drums, thickly lined with mud, for fear the ones he found on arrival would not produce the heat he needed.

These inter-family banquets were always extremely formal. Everyone dressed well, and observed the accepted etiquette of behavior and conventions. The younger members of our clan arrived first, and the seating was always according to certain rules: the most honored or venerable guests faced the door; the host sat on the far side opposite them. Men did not necessarily alternate with women; it was not unusual for the men to be on one side and the women on the other; the men, however, sat on the women's right, as being the place of honor.

We children, of course, made ourselves scarce on these occasions, pretending to be both silent and invisible, eating what was given us, and not reaching across the table to pick a favorite morsel ourselves; and we had to finish every grain of rice and scrap of food. When we went to dine with a relative, it was altogether different: company manners required that we leave food on our plates to show how generous our host had been—we had been given more than enough—and being replete, we had naturally been obliged to send the plate away with some of his bounty still on it.

My mother never made any observations about food in a restaurant, but if we had been to dine at the home of one of my father's sisters, she would always have much to say: "Ah——!" she would begin. "Not enough to eat! And how strange to serve only three *ch'ao* dishes instead of four—most unusual. Then what possessed them to serve the fish in the middle, instead of at the end; the shrimp, too, were not well done, and quite out of place. I really much prefer to see some food left on the table, otherwise I feel I may have skimped something. After all, they have no need to be so frugal. Well, at least it can never be said that anyone goes away hungry from our home."

My mother's eagle eye noticed everything, and she would always be sure to comment on it. Added to her energy, it ensured that the house was spotlessly clean and arranged with meticulous symmetry: nothing was ever out of place, untidy or dirty. At the center of every activity, there she was, plainly and simply gowned, her hair pulled back into a neat bun; at one moment at her embroidery—throughout my childhood I never wore shoes she had not embellished with her needle— at another, making exquisite baby clothes for my sisters' children. She did everything well, especially cooking. She prepared her own soy sauce, to which she sometimes added shrimp eggs—a complicated process of extracting the eggs, drying them, and mixing them with the soy; she also made the duck sauce in preference to using the commercial kind. If she was old-fashioned, it was with all the old-fashioned virtues of patience and industry. And yet my mother still found time to read; her knowledge of the classics was unusual for a lady of her day; and like my father, she loved old histories and novels, turning the pages of the beautiful wood-block books, printed on rice paper and bound with thread. My Number Two sister and I are the only ones who resemble her in our passion for neatness in housekeeping: the rest of my family, it must be confessed, are terrible housekeepers.

While my mother busied herself with innumerable duties, such as deciding whether the room in which food was stored was at the right temperature and had a suitable draft of air, or seeing to the proper disposition of the flour, rice and wine, my father was equally occupied, if in a more hedonistic way.

61

His plants were a primary consideration: even when the Japanese occupation, after 1937, gradually made it more and more difficult to get any fuel to heat the house, he insisted on keeping the fires stoked for the hothouses. And now, in April, he exercised a great deal of care over his *bonsai*, as well as directing the gardeners concerning the cultivation of spring flowers and the preparation of the plants to follow in sequence in the courtyard flowerbeds in summer and autumn.

My father loved to read, as I have said, and still writes, in his nineties, a beautiful Chinese script, betraying not the slightest tremor of the brush. I would see him in his study, poring over his stamp collection, with magnifying glass and tweezers, or tinkering with locks; and he was continually repairing the watches and clocks to be found in the living quarters and reception rooms. Whether he succeeded in putting them together again, or making them go once more, I have no idea, but he enjoyed doing things with his hands. Most of all, he was devoted to the art of living, which extended to every aspect of his activities. He liked to eat the best food, although he was not a large eater, and was slight, never weighing more than a hundred and ten pounds. He held the view that if one ate the best, one did not need so much. He always had an aperitif before dinner, and wine with it, and sometimes a liqueur to follow, and yet I never saw him at all discomposed with drinking, as he was moderate in all things. But he certainly knew how to live: even his tobacco had *kuei-hua* flowers marinated in cognac added to it, to impart a more delicate aroma. Characteristically, he had retired at the age of forty-five, before I was born, to devote himself to the joys of leisure. Not that the calls upon his time had ever been excessive: there had always been managers for the stores, factories and cinemas we owned in Peking, Tientsin and Wu-hsi.

Both my parents loved the Chinese opera so much that they

had season tickets, attended it regularly in Peking, and sometimes went to hear it in Tientsin or as far afield as Shanghai. They preferred, I think, the opera house not far from us, in Tung-an Shih-ch'ang, the famous bazaar (just as the Covent Garden Opera House in London is to be found in Covent Garden Market, only it was, if anything, much more varied and elaborate). One could snuff the scent of the beautiful fresh fruit miles away; the shops offered everything from flowers, birds and pets of all kinds, to yard goods and the handmade velvet blossoms we wore at the New Year, and there were elegant cafés and restaurants as well. Many people, like my parents, made their way there for tea in the afternoon, went shopping, and afterwards dined there before going to the opera.

While our elders, as I have pointed out, lived in some degree of magnificence, and the children were brought up in a completely sheltered environment, we, the youngest, were not exactly pampered, and I was conscious sometimes of the difference. Whereas our parents slept in silken sheets, spread with covers of the finest flannel, we had to be content with cotton. Our undergarments were made of the same unsympathetic material, stiffly starched: so hard, that where the neckband of an undershift had to show above the blue collar of the jacket (worn much higher than it is today) it cut an angry red mark in our necks. In winter, these rigid, freezing shifts, topped by their unrelenting halters, were especially uncomfortable. If I complained to my *amah*, she simply replied that it was by my mother's order, and that ended the matter.

The contrast between luxury and austerity was also noticeable in the life lived by our servants. On freezing winter mornings—not until April did they yield to warmer days—we used to see the menservants washing the upper part of their bodies from a bucket of hot water, afterwards emptying it on the ground to help thaw the ice on the stone-paved courtyard. We saw them, just as we remarked with an incurious eye the snow-covered forms in the narrow alleys as we sped to school, which the rickshaw boy would explain were the bodies of beggars who had died from cold or hunger, or both: we accepted them, without drawing any moral conclusions, as natural phenomena. Even when the boy would call our attention with a grin to the people with cigarettes in their mouths, pointed skyward—anti-aircraft guns as they were called—and told us they were heroin addicts, we viewed them with interest, but without apperception or sympathy.

Surprisingly enough, we never had dancing lessons, although we all somehow learned to dance well. When I was little, I did not go out much, and certainly not to chaperoned parties until I went to college. The various sports gave one an opportunity to meet young people of one's own age, and during my college years I went out, always chaperoned, to dinners and dances with approved young men. My escort was always expected to call on my parents first, which must have been something of an ordeal. After entering the main gate, he would be conducted to them, and announced by a manservant in a loud voice as a friend of Miss Number Seven daughter, and a formal exchange of greetings would ensue. After I had been invited a number of times, I might be permitted to go out with him, and when I returned I was questioned about the evening and the hapless young man—who were his parents? where did they live? what were their connections?—a questionnaire elaborate and embarrassing enough to discourage any suitor, had I forced myself to itemize it to him, and upon which they had presumably satisfied themselves before I had gone out.

In those days it was fashionable, and advanced, to go to the cabarets which had dance hostesses, or to the finest hotels, such as the Grand Hôtel de Pékin, which was under French management and considered the most distinguished. It had three orchestras, or "swing bands" as they were called, and all the musicians were Filipinos. No Western performers were in Peking at that time nor did any Chinese play Occidental dance instruments. The ballroom was beautiful and I loved to go there. Nevertheless, it was not accepted as proper for a well brought up young Chinese girl to dance in public with a man, and on one occasion an uncle of mine saw me and expressed his shocked disapproval to my elder brother. Those of my sisters who were already in society attended charity balls as a matter of course, but only to cut ribbons or sell tickets: to take part was quite a different story.

One of the young men I knew during my third year at college had a white-topped convertible sports car, which he drove himself; he also played polo. All this added up to quite a number of black marks in my parents' eyes. The possession of a convertible, driven without a chauffeur, and polo playing, were considered to indicate a remarkable degree of profligacy; my friend was clearly no good—a playboy—and the acquaintanceship, innocent enough, was firmly discouraged.

INTERLUDE

*Of Foods for Drinking—
a Cocktail Party Adapted
from a Mandarin Table*

ONE FORM OF ENTERTAINMENT was unknown in the family circle of my youth: the cocktail party. In the first place, wines, liqueurs or spirits as understood in China were always regarded as an agreeable adjunct to good food, and not the other way around. *Mah jong* parties involved serving a light collation—nuts, tea pastries—washed down with a choice tea, and no one ever gave parties for the sole purpose of drinking. Not that my countrymen did not have a keen enjoyment of wines, but they would have thought it barbarous to be helplessly intoxicated or to drink to the point of being unable to appreciate a fine dinner. To be amiably tipsy was one thing; to be drunk would be to lose face.

In spite of this national trait of sobriety and moderation, the versatility of the Chinese repertoire is perfectly capable of supplying tidbits in harmony with a Western cocktail party:

Butterfly Shrimp	Spring Rolls
Five-spiced Spareribs,	Shrimp Balls
Peking Style	Meatballs
Sesame Seed Chicken	Shrimp Toast

This array would certainly tempt the appetite and awaken the taste buds, and have the added merit, from the Chinese point of view, of "matching" the drinks served. Nothing further is needed by way of embellishment for these delicacies than to present them to your guests on separate, beautiful, and warmed plates.

BUTTERFLY SHRIMP
SU HSIA-JEN

This recipe produces a delicately flavored appetizer in a light, crisp casing.

12 large shrimp or prawns,
    fresh or fresh-frozen
¼ cup Chinese rice wine
    or dry sherry
pinch of salt
pinch of sugar
shredded cabbage leaves
cottonseed oil

BATTER
1 cup all-purpose flour
1 cup cornstarch
1 egg
½ teaspoon salt
2 tablespoons cottonseed
    oil
1 tablespoon Chinese white
    vinegar
1 heaping teaspoon baking
    soda
¼ cup cold water

Shell and devein the shrimp, and with a knife or cleaver "butterfly" by cutting them in half for most of their length. You can, if you wish, leave the tails on, as a part to hold when they are served. Dip them in the rice wine, to which the salt and sugar have been added. Beat all the other ingredients in a bowl to make a thin, flowing batter. Coat each shrimp evenly all over with the batter. Heat a *wok* and fill with sufficient oil to deep-fry. Heat the oil to bubbling, add the coated shrimp, and reduce the heat to low immediately. After thirty seconds, turn one shrimp. If it is a golden brown underneath, turn all the pieces and continue to deep-fry for an equivalent length of time, so that all are beautifully colored on both sides. Remove from the *wok* and place on a bed of shredded cabbage leaves (these help to absorb any surplus oil). Let the shrimp rest a little to firm them up; then serve them while they are hot.

FIVE-SPICED SPARERIBS, PEKING STYLE
WU-HSIANG P'AI-KU

2 pounds spareribs
1 teaspoon salt
½ teaspoon saltpeter
2 tablespoons *hoisin* sauce
4 slices fresh ginger root,
  ⅛ inch thick

4 green scallions
1 tablespoon rice wine or
  dry sherry
2 tablespoons pale soy sauce
1 tablespoon honey or sugar

Separate the spareribs and chop into pieces one and a quarter inches long. Combine the salt and saltpeter and rub each piece with the mixture. Let the meat stand for twenty-four hours.

Prepare a barbecue sauce by combining the *hoisin* sauce, ginger, green scallions, wine and soy sauce. Heat the oven to 375 degrees, place the spareribs on a rack with a drip pan underneath, and brush on the sauce. Bake for thirty-five to forty minutes. Glaze lightly with the honey, or the sugar in solution, and serve hot.

SESAME SEED CHICKEN
CHIH-MA CHI

2 whole chicken breasts,
  skinned

⅛ teaspoon salt (scant)
1 egg (white only)

71

sesame seeds   vegetable oil

Each breast should be chopped into five pieces, across the length, and dipped into white of egg to which the salt has been added. Sprinkle all over with sesame seed and deep-fry rapidly—about one minute—in hot cottonseed oil. This method should not be despised for its extreme simplicity.

SPRING ROLLS
CH'UN CHÜAN

24 spring roll skins   1 lightly beaten egg

Separate the skins, placing the soft, not the fried side up. Brush all around the edges of each skin with the egg. Place the chosen filling (see below) on the lower third of the skin, and roll, tucking in the edges to square off the shape, and sealing with the brushed-egg edges to form little rolls with blunt ends.

Deep-fry the spring roll skins in very hot oil (375 degrees), pushing each roll down into the oil and cooking for about six minutes, turning once, until golden-brown. Drain and serve immediately with one of the following: soy sauce, or a mixture of Chinese vinegar and hot pepper oil, or a sweet and sour sauce (I prefer the plain soy sauce). The roll is dipped into the sauce and eaten with the fingers, or if one wants smaller tidbits, sliced in half and speared with a toothpick.

FILLINGS: Usually the fillings are made of equal amounts of three main ingredients, such as ham, black mushrooms and bamboo shoots, coarsely chopped, to which small quantities of bean sprouts may be added. Pork may be included instead of ham, in a tripartite combination of Chinese chives, pork and bean sprouts. Shrimp is not used. The mixture should be lightly stir-fried (ch'ao), with a pinch of salt, and drained dry

72

before using. About a quarter of a pound of the filling is sufficient for twenty-four rolls.

The skins themselves, extremely thin, translucent pancakes, are made of plain flour and water, but as they are difficult to make, it is usual to buy them, about fifty at a time. They are prepared to the right size, eight inches across and circular. As the name implies, they are always associated with springtime in China, but are equally good to eat at any time of the year.

SHRIMP BALLS
CHA HSIA-CH'IU

1 pound fresh shrimp	white part only
¼ pound water chestnuts, finely chopped	1 tablespoon Chinese rice wine or light dry sherry
1 egg	½ teaspoon salt
½ teaspoon mashed ginger root	dash of pepper
1 finely chopped scallion,	1 tablespoon flour
	vegetable oil

Chop the shelled and deveined shrimp and the water chestnuts almost to a paste. Mix with all the other ingredients thoroughly. It is helpful to refrigerate the mixture until it is firm. Form it into balls by squeezing as much as you can hold in your thumb and first two fingers through the top of your right fist, and scoop up with a spoon dipped in cold water, using the left hand. Put each ball into a *wok* filled to within two inches of the top with cottonseed oil heated to bubbling (375 degrees). The balls sink to the bottom, and float to the surface when they are done. Test one, and if the ball is spongy to the touch, the meat inside is cooked, while the outside should be a golden brown. The cooking time is two to three

73

minutes. The quantities given will make from twelve to fourteen balls (depending upon the size), which should be served piping hot.

Similar in preparation, although quite different in flavor, are meatballs, Chinese style. There is not too much advance work, and the cooking time is relatively short, making them ideal for cocktail entertaining. This recipe makes from ten to twelve small meatballs.

MEATBALLS

CHA JOU WAN-TZU

1 pound finely chopped
   pork, not too lean
2 lightly mixed egg whites
pinch of salt
2 pieces finely chopped
   scallions (white part)

1 teaspoon pounded ginger
   root
pinch of monosodium
   glutamate
½ cup cold water
2 cups vegetable oil

Mix all the ingredients thoroughly. Form the balls in the same way as the shrimp balls. The slipperiness of the egg whites helps in the formation of the round shape, and also aids in preventing the meatballs from sticking together while cooking. For cocktail parties the balls should be about one inch in diameter. Heat a *wok*, and put in sufficient vegetable oil, at least two cups, to deep-fry. The oil should be brought to low heat, or the balls will be hard outside, and not cooked within. Avoid sesame oil, which is too strongly flavored. Deep-fry for approximately fifteen minutes, turning frequently, until a golden brown all over. These meatballs can be further enhanced with a dipping salt, *hua-chiao yen,* made of *ch'ao*-cooked star anise, salt and Szechwan peppercorns.

DIPPING SALT (*hua-chiao yen*)   peppercorns
5 tablespoons salt   2 pieces star anise
1 tablespoon Szechwan

Put all the ingredients whole into a skillet over high heat, and turn the heat down to moderate at once, stirring rapidly until the mixture browns lightly—about five minutes. It needs careful watching, as it burns easily. Remove from the skillet and pound the mixture with a pestle in a mortar, and sieve into a bowl. These quantities make about a quarter of a cup. The mixture is pungent, and guests should be warned to use it sparingly.

Finally, a savory morsel I well remember eating in Peking, which makes an attractive snack or appetizer and presents few difficulties in the making:

SHRIMP TOAST
HSIA-JEN T'U-SSU

½ pound fresh shrimp   ½ teaspoon salt
1 loaf white bread   2 cups cottonseed oil
1 tablespoon Chinese rice   garnish: shredded Virginia
   wine or dry sherry   ham and fresh Chinese
2 egg whites   parsley
1 tablespoon cornstarch

Shell and devein the shrimp; mince fine. Slice the white bread very thinly, cutting each piece diagonally to make four triangles; cut off the crusts. Three slices are sufficient. Mix all the remaining ingredients together, except the ham and the parsley, to make a smooth paste. Spread the mixture on the bread triangles with a knife or spatula and put a little Virginia ham and one leaf of Chinese parsley on each for flavor and an attractive color contrast. Heat a *wok*, put in the oil, and heat it to 375 degrees; deep-fry the pieces shrimp side down. The ham and parsley will adhere to the paste. After fifty seconds, turn, and fry the other side.

Any of these appetizers might be served separately in a Western-style menu, as *hors d'oeuvre* at lunch or dinner, or even as an impromptu snack at midnight. Provided one has the ingredients, all of these dishes, with the exception of the spareribs, can be prepared within a matter of minutes, and are eaten just as quickly.

For the guests who stay behind there are foods which are less easy to hand around, but nevertheless make an attractive snack or collation.

In the chapter "Third Moon" I mentioned a favorite family dish, *mu-shi jou*, a pork preparation eaten in characteristic northern style, wrapped in pancakes, which is too good to be ignored.

STIRRED EGG AND PORK WITH PANCAKES
MU-SHI JOU

¼ pound pork loin, slightly marbled, thinly sliced against the grain

1 generous tablespoon cottonseed oil

1 tablespoon Chinese rice wine or dry sherry

2 ounces dried wooden ear fungus

2 ounces dried tiger lily buds ("golden needles")

2 cups chicken stock (see page 49)

4 well-beaten eggs

3 long scallions, chopped

1 tablespoon soy sauce

1 or 2 drops sesame seed oil

PANCAKES (*pao-ping*)

4 cups all-purpose wheat flour

1½ cups hot water

sesame seed oil

76

Make the pancakes first. Add the water to the flour slowly and mix until the dough has a springy texture. Flour a board lightly and knead the dough with the ball of the hand for three or four minutes. Cover the dough and let it rest for about ten minutes. Then divide it in half and roll each half into a cylinder fifteen or sixteen inches long. Slice each cylinder into rounds one inch thick and flatten each with the ball of your hand. Brush the top of the rounds with sesame seed oil and join them in pairs, sandwich-style, oiled sides in. Then, on a floured board, roll out each sandwich-pancake into a thin seven-inch circle. Preheat a well-seasoned skillet (do not grease it) and over low heat cook each sandwich-pancake for three or four minutes on each side. Remove from the skillet and pull the two halves of the pancake apart. The pancakes can be made ahead of time and frozen until required.

Presoak the wooden ear in lukewarm water for one hour (or let it stand overnight in water), and rinse to ensure that no sand or grit remains in it; then drain.

First simmer the wooden ear and the tiger lily buds in the chicken stock for five or six minutes; then drain. Meanwhile warm a *wok* and in it heat the cottonseed oil to 375 degrees, making sure the oil is spread over the sides. Put the pork and the rice wine into the *wok*, and stir-fry for two or three minutes. Drain, remove the pork, and squeeze all the oil out of it.

Pour the eggs into the *wok* and stir-fry quickly, adding almost immediately the pork, scallions, soy sauce, sesame seed oil, wooden ear and tiger lily buds. Continue to stir-fry rapidly for thirty to sixty seconds to blend the flavors; then serve. It is almost impossible to give the exact timing for the stir-frying as there is considerable variation from one stove to another. The eggs in this recipe should be just barely set when one adds the other ingredients. Take care to put them into the *wok* in the order given; if not, the wooden ear will have disintegrated.

The *mu-shi* pork is brought to the table on a serving dish, and the pancakes, kept warm in a napkin, on a separate plate. Each guest brushes a little plum sauce on a pancake, with a few slivers of scallion, and puts some of the filling into the center. The pancake is then rolled up into a plump tube, with one end tucked in. It is agreeably luscious to eat by hand, and pleasantly difficult to keep all the filling in, if one has been greedy over the quantity.

FOURTH MOON

In view of the importance of the family, marriage, birth and death occupy a peculiarly significant place in the rituals of Chinese life. Many customs that prevailed in my time have been discontinued, although they must have left their mark on those who knew them.

Already, when I was growing up, the custom of the matchmaker had ceased to concern us, although careful consideration was still given by my parents to the mating of suitable couples, in accord with their age, rank, and fortune, and with the time of day, and the year in the cycle of twelve, when they were born. No matchmaker would consider bringing together a man and a woman born in the Year of the Horse, as horses will never share the same trough; and it would clearly be unwise for one born in the Year of the Sheep to marry a man who was, so to say, Tiger-born. Once these weighty considerations had been threshed out, invitations were dispatched by the son's parents on red paper: no indication of an r.s.v.p. was included, and it was always understood that the invitation extended to cover the whole family to whom it was sent.

One charming story handed down in our family concerns the engagement of my father's brother. When the matchmaker had compiled the customary horoscope of the young girl she was to submit as a suitable bride (which included her year sign, the date and hour of her birth, as well as minute particulars of her rank, connections and dowry, and was accompanied by a portrait), she also dispatched to him one of the girl's delicately embroidered shoes, only three inches long, for a small foot was regarded as the quintessence of beauty.

When my uncle saw the shoe, or rather, tiny slippers, he exclaimed that he had no need to look further. Brushing aside the vermilion envelope containing the genealogical data so carefully compiled by the matchmaker, he declared that whoever owned and wore such a shoe must be the most beautiful girl in Peking. Fortunately for my uncle, his bride was as lovely as her shoes were small, and the arrangements were brought to a happy conclusion.

Since several hundred guests commonly sat down to a wedding banquet, arrangements for the ceremony were usually made at a restaurant, as was the case with the weddings of three of my elder sisters. Nowadays the style is usually to marry in church or chapel and serve a twelve-course banquet at a restaurant afterwards.

Naturally many preliminaries led up to the ceremony itself. I remember that one of my sisters used to be taken out by her fiancé, formally chaperoned by my other sisters, and they had to return at a fixed time from their innocuous outing in Pei Hai. The future son-in-law had also to pay a formal call on his prospective in-laws, at which the family all inspected him from behind a screen, with much subdued whispering and giggling; and he was expected to send, among other gifts, a goose, dyed red, for his bride, although geese were not eaten in Peking: the gift was purely symbolic of marital happiness. All the expenses of the wedding were borne by the bridegroom's family—no mean outlay, for the festivities lasted three days and guests would stay in our house for a week.

There was no end to the bustle and activity in both households. I recall our tailor hard at work for months—we all had to have new clothes, from the oldest to the youngest.

The wedding arrangements had to be made by a woman with specific qualifications: she was expected to be married, with at least one son and one daughter, and have her parents still living—all indications of good luck, insuring that the couple would be fruitful. I have acted in this capacity myself, as I fulfilled the necessary conditions. The role requires that one oversee all the arrangements, such as choosing the most auspicious day and hour; shopping for any necessaries, even selecting and placing the furniture; and most particularly, preparing the marriage bed: putting a red net bag, containing five hard-boiled red eggs, beneath the pillow. Among other symbolic acts expected of me were hiding a pair of chopsticks —punning on their name, *k'uai-tzu*, that is, "hurry up" (and have sons); and offering the couple lotus seeds, *lien-tzu*, which means "continue," or in other words, always have boys.

In olden days the bride was carried from her home to the ceremony in a quilted red palanquin ornamented with gold and silver, and wore a red dress with a red veil over her head. The date was chosen from the Huang Li, the calendar dating back to the first Emperor of China, and one never married at night or in the early morning. A rainy day was considered unlucky, and the death of any member of the family always caused a long postponement. Our family was already more modern, and my sisters were married in Western-style dresses, although other traditional customs, such as the dowry and the banquet, were observed.

Most weddings I attended were civil ceremonies held in a hotel. At one end of the room was a platform, with a long altar covered with a richly embroidered cloth. On it were two large red candles in pewter or cloisonné holders, and an incense burner in the middle, and behind were hangings with wedding symbols. Flowers, growing in pots, arranged symmetrically, added color. The wedding certificate lay on a table, ready to be sealed by all the main participants.

The official who performed the ceremony was always some-one of high position. Two matchmakers were also present. They were not real matchmakers, but were also people of rank, and had a purely honorary function, that of standing beside the fathers of the bride and groom. There was, in ad-dition, a master of ceremonies, who introduced everyone on the platform. One side of it was allocated to the bride's family, the other to the groom's. The attendants included two groomsmen, a best man, a flower girl and a ring girl.

After the wedding march, the master of ceremonies began the introductions and those introduced bowed to each other three times, and the officials and matchmakers took turns in making complimentary speeches. The ladies, however, were silent throughout. The ceremony of stamping the marriage certificate with the chops (seals) of the witnesses, after the exchange of rings, concluded the ceremony, and there fol-lowed an endless series of formal photographs.

The dinner served at a wedding was most elaborate. The highly polished round tables were first of all laid out with cold appetizers, arranged in one of two ways, either on one large plate, with many varieties in even numbers, or on four smaller plates, with two combinations of appetizers on each. The individual preparations were made with great artistry, appearing in the guise of a phoenix, a flower, an animal, or a fish, and contrasted in color, shape, texture and flavor. These beautifully decorated plates were made of such foods as cold chicken, cold spiced beef, thousand-year eggs, pickled cu-cumber, black mushrooms, jellyfish salad, pickled Chinese cabbage, and cold ham from Chin-hua or Yunnan—all trans-formed into exotic beasts by the skill of the chef.

Next appeared four light dishes, stir-fried (ch'ao) and rapidly cooked, such as shrimp Shanghai, sautéed pork, chicken variously seasoned, pork kidney delicately scored to procure the maximum tenderness, and abalone or sea cucumber. Naturally these were cooked according to complicated methods of preparation, and combined with spices and flavors to bring out the most delicate nuances of taste.

For the most important course, Peking duck or shark fin was served, for which there had been days of preparation. Shark fin alone had to be carefully chosen for size and freshness, then delicately peeled, soaked in water for three days (the water was constantly changed); protected by a bamboo frame so that it would not disintegrate, it was simmered for four or five hours to clean it thoroughly, simmered again with wine to remove any trace of fishy smell, and finally cooked in a bouillon containing a whole chicken cut in pieces and some Chin-hua ham. The bouillon itself had been reduced over a medium fire for three hours. The finishing touch was a slow cooking of all the ingredients together for ten minutes to enable the various flavors to penetrate and pervade the shark fin.

A whole fish, set upright on a carefully warmed platter and surrounded by a gleaming sauce, as though still swimming in its native element, served, as it were, as an epilogue or at least as a signal that the end was approaching. There remained to be considered a refreshing soup, such as stuffed cucumber, and possibly four delicate rice dishes, that is, dishes appropriate for serving with rice, such as bite-sized pieces of chicken, steamed, and then rapidly crisp-fried, preserving the skin for its delicious taste; rich pieces of pork shoulder, dipped in a highly seasoned sauce; young squid, chosen by their miniature size for tenderness—they decorated the dish of bean sprouts on which they were served like tiny stars; pork, red-cooked with soy to the essence of its savor, and served with a Szechwan delicacy, fish sauce—fresh fish, apart from carp, being an almost unknown commodity in Szechwan, and in contrast, a dish of vegetables, such as black mushrooms and Chinese chard, embellished according to the whim and artistry of the chef.

At such a large meal, the wedding guests would not, of course, eat large portions: they confined themselves to one or two mouthfuls of each dish. The table was laid with a small plate of blue and white porcelain, chosen for its beauty, on which small bones could be placed, and beside it a soup bowl and porcelain soup spoon: these did not necessarily match if they were antique, and were no less treasured on that account; and I remember that my family was suitably impressed on finding that none of the china matched at the home of one of my brother's wives.

The only other items at each place were chopsticks of silver and ivory, and a small wine cup. The wine, carefully warmed, was poured from silver wine vessels resembling teapots. Tea was never served at the table, although tiny cups of red tea, such as *p'u-erh*, dark and strong, were offered afterwards to clear the palate, or as a digestive or liqueur, in a separate room.

When the wedding night arrives, there is often quite a lot of horseplay. Sticky sweetmeats made of glutinous rice cooked with sugar, and flavored with the preserved yellow petals of the *kuei-hua*, are wrapped in red paper and offered to the couple; and sometimes, egged on by the eldest brother, the Number One son, pranksters will hide under the bed, or make a loud noise with firecrackers outside the windows, or sit in the bridal chamber and refuse to leave until the groom kisses the bride in public. This is most embarrassing for them because public demonstrations of affection are not considered proper. The following day the bride rises early to prepare tea for her mother-in-law, to demonstrate she is a good wife and now a daughter of the house; and one week later she is allowed to return to her family for three days, after which her husband calls to take her back.

In a family of good standing the bride always took enough clothes with her to last two years, as well as a carefully approved array of jewelry. In order to avoid losing face by not supplying an adequate dowry, her family might have to borrow money to buy the trousseau, and be plunged into debt for years. In the old days, wedding gifts were sent only to the bridegroom, and the bride received gifts afterwards, during the first month, when she might visit relatives and close friends: at this time she would be given money in little red envelopes. It was also customary to hire people to acknowledge the gifts with letters of thanks sent out on red cards. It then only remained for the new wife to learn the ways of the family of which she now formed a part, and raise up sons.

The birth of a son was always the signal for rejoicing, and the young mother now enjoyed a superior status. Red eggs, symbols of the happy event, were dispatched in all directions: the future of the family was assured. Birthdays are celebrated only at one month, for the first son; and at one year old, and thereafter every tenth year. Big celebrations are usually held at a man's forty-ninth, or as we Chinese would consider it, on his fiftieth birthday; but girls' birthdays were of no account, and passed by without parties, gifts, or notice of any kind. Babies wore tiny aprons, called *tou-tou*, to protect their navels, which were thought to be particularly vulnerable to cold: the boys' was slightly longer than the girls'; and at one month the head was shaved, leaving a tuft to protect the soft spot where the bones meet. Henceforth the newborn was in the charge of his wet nurse, a peasant woman who often gave away her own child to care for him and would continue to look after him even after he was weaned.

Those were all happy moments; but I was soon made aware

that there were darker hours. At the time of which I am writing, funerals in China were accompanied by rites which I still remember with a shudder. People of position were obliged to summon Buddhist monks to recite prayers for the dead relative, whose coffin was placed either in the house, with the family and children watching over it in turns, or on a temple altar. The temples were dirty, like the priests who served in them, and dark and shadowy, lighted only by tiny candles. Two fearsome gods, Heng and Ha, whose duties were to chase away evil spirits, guarded either side of the entrance. The monks were extremely expensive to hire, although it was necessary, in order to show fitting respect for the dead, to employ numbers of them; and families were often reduced to debt to fulfill their obligations.

The monks endlessly droned the Lotus sutra in an incomprehensible monotone, to the accompaniment of wooden clappers. For the first thirty days of mourning, men were supposed not to shave, and everyone in any degree of consanguinity was required to wear coarse, off-white garments, unseamed, with ties instead of buttons. Then for one year, clothes had to be gray, and of cotton, and no make-up could be worn. Following a period of gray, black was permissible. Mourning clothes were worn for six years if one's parents died and the death of a father or grandfather always brought marriage arrangements to a halt.

The funeral procession I also remember with horror. Figures were carried in the cortège that were made out of paper —*papier-mâché*—representing the deceased, his servants, and all his household furniture; sometimes the bizarre note of a paper automobile was included: all these were designed to accompany the dead to his last resting-place and impress the bystanders with his wealth and importance. The corpse was carried on a hearse covered with a quilted cloth and borne by sixteen men, and the entire family of mourners had to walk for miles on foot with it to the grave. There all the paper objects were burned, together with paper money, so that the dead would be well provided for. Children's funerals were especially heartbreaking—there were models of all the toys the child had loved. When a young sister of mine died at the age of six, my mother was prostrated with grief, and carried offerings of food and toys to her tomb for a hundred days, which was considered an excessive demonstration of sorrow.

As with marriages, the auspicious day for the funeral had to be decided by the *feng-shui hsien-sheng*, the geomancer of the "spirit of wind and water," who would decide the right day and hour, as well as the correct land to buy for the tomb, and its proper orientation. The *feng-shui hsien-sheng* was consulted at many points: he could tell where a house should be built; he would notice that a chimney on a neighboring house was exerting evil influences, and might suggest that a mirror placed in a strategic position would reflect the evil back whence it came. He would even suggest auspicious days for taking baths: since it was important to retain oils in the body, one had to be careful. Even the moment for a haircut, because it meant losing something from the body, could be significant.

Naturally a funeral, which brought together many relatives, also served as an occasion for a banquet, but one entirely of vegetables: of twelve courses, nevertheless, but not even one egg might be used in the preparations. Bean curd provided all kinds of shapes and textures to mimic the appearance of meats. Some was of the dried kind, some fried and rolled, after drying, into sheets, and intricately layered; some rolled into balls. In former days some preserved vegetables were used on these occasions, but in the main they were fresh. Turnips, very white and juicy, were a favorite. Walnuts and ginkgo nuts were served, but in the north no peanuts or almonds appeared as in Cantonese cuisine. *Fan-tzu*, the transparent noodles, were another ingredient used, and in Canton the "hair" vegetable was popular. The banquet, called *su-hsi* (*su* means vegetable), is largely ceremonial, and in spite of the large number of dishes, people do not eat very much of them. No desserts, such as are served between courses on other banquet occasions, were ever served at these funeral wakes; they were considered too frivolous for the circumstances.

To come full circle, one should mention that the complimentary gift to a male relative on his birthday—such as a man celebrates on his forty-ninth—is to offer him a dish of *shou-nien*, or "long life" noodles. These are never cut, and correspond to the Occidental birthday cake. The symbolism is of course obvious.

INTERLUDE
Of Peking Duck

No DOUBT MOST OF THE RITES AND CEREMONIES I have described have been discontinued in the new China, although they are still practiced in Taiwan and in Chinese communities overseas. The continuity of the family ensured the preservation of customs, which lasted as long as the whole framework of Chinese life remained intact. In retrospect, I think there was too much needless extravagance and display at both wedding and funeral ceremonies, as exemplified in the bridal procession, in which the dowry was ostentatiously paraded so that the awed bystanders might count the trunks of clothing and estimate the wealth of the parents; or in the funeral preparations, which often temporarily beggared the relatives of the deceased. At least at weddings there was gaiety, excitement, color and noise, as well as beauty, if one did not count the cost, and the wedding banquet was an opportunity to display the consummate artistry of the head chef.

Festivities like these were an integral part of my childhood, and even now I like to reproduce some of the dishes which formed a part of our family celebrations.

Although I have mentioned that Peking duck appeared as one course at formal banquets, it was not unusual to devote an entire meal to it. Two restaurants, Chuan Chu Teh and Pien Yi Fang, on Ch'ien Men Ta Chieh (Front Gate Street), were famous for duck, although many other restaurants in Peking prepared it.

Restaurants specializing in duck—nothing else was served —were almost invariably owned and run by Mohammedans, as their religion forbade them to touch pork. Rows and rows of ducks hung from the ceiling and these establishments tended to be generally greasy; but one went there for the duck and not for the décor.

The Peking duck dinner, as served at the Chuan Chu Teh, really began with the raising of the birds. The carefully selected young birds were raised in fenced enclosures so small that they had no room to walk about, and were fed a little at a time, often with millet and sorghum, until they grew fat and lazy. They were not allowed to get too big or too old: a six-pound bird was the desideratum, although a seven- to eight-pound bird is more usual in the United States.

As soon as one is killed, a bamboo tube is inserted just below the neck (or under the wing) and the bird's skin gradually separates from the flesh as air is blown into the tube. In the old days this was done by mouth; today it is quicker to use a bicycle pump. When sufficient air has been blown in, the neck and vent are tied up to prevent the collapse of the skin, and the duck is then hung up to dry. In the past this was done by hanging the bird in a draft, and leaving it for more than twenty-four hours. The duck is coated with honey, without any seasoning. The skin, now tight and shiny, completely separates from the meat. When the cook adjudges the bird ready for cooking, it is placed in a hot oven and roasted for one hour: less in China, as charcoal is generally used, which generates a greater heat. The duck has to hang in the oven to allow the fat to drip down, and this must be saved, as it contributes a special ingredient to one of the courses.

When one arrived at the restaurant there was naturally some delay before one's dinner was ready, so that a convivial period of nut munching and wine drinking usually preceded the food. The duck was always carved by the cook in front of the guests; first the skin, and then the meat. The skin, regarded as the choicest part, was now a delicate, deep, translucent brown, crisp and luscious. Next arrived a plate of *pao-ping*, the special Peking pancakes in which duck is wrapped. One spread these with *hoisin* (duck) sauce and scallions, which had been laboriously trimmed to leave only the white part, blossoming into a tassel at either end, and put some duck meat on top, rolled up the pancake, and ate the ambrosial combination. No limit, incidentally, was placed on the number of ducks eaten; the more duck, the better the soup one would finally consume. After the meat followed an egg course, at which point the duck fat came into its own, and contributed richly to the steamed custard-like dish.

Finally the soup arrived, made of the duck bones and Chinese cabbage—a splendid conclusion. After so much rich eating it was customary to serve the strong red tea called *p'u-erh ch'a*, to cleanse the palate. Such duck dinners as these were always for special parties, at which friends were entertained, and were not arranged for family gatherings, since children, at any rate those in our circle, were not taken to late dinners in restaurants.

Some Chinese gourmets, my father and my brothers-in-law among them, liked to eat the strongly flavored oil sacs in the tail of the bird, but it is more usual to discard this part, as it is decidedly an acquired taste. And in general, although duck is eaten at all times, one did not have it in the summer, as being altogether too rich and heating for the blood.

Peking duck can be made at home, if one is prepared to take the time and trouble: I think it is well worth it.

PEKING DUCK
PEI-CHING K'AO-YA

1 fresh ranch duck, 7½ to
  8 pounds

1 tablespoon cornstarch
1 tablespoon honey

FIRST COATING
4 cups boiling water
1 teaspoon baking soda

8–10 scallions (white part
  only)
hoisin (duck) sauce

SECOND COATING
2 cups boiling water

pancakes (see recipe, page
  76)

First prepare the pancakes and refrigerate until required.

Clean and wash the duck, cut the tips of the wings off, and remove the tail sacs. Tie off the neck and vent openings and insert the tube of a bicycle pump under the skin near the neck opening. Pump the air in gently, to detach the skin from the flesh.

Prepare the first coating by mixing the boiling water and soda. Put a hook through the neck of the bird above the tie, and holding the bird by the hook over a *wok*, brush the solution on thoroughly and completely. Hang up to dry for three hours.

Next, mix the second coating by combining the boiling water and cornstarch; then add the honey. Hold the bird over the *wok* once again and ladle the solution over the duck thoroughly.

Now hang the duck in the wind, out of the sun for twenty-four hours, or in the draft made by an electric fan. The skin will now have a brittle, papery texture. To roast the duck, preheat the oven to 475 degrees, place the bird breast up on a turkey rack with a drip pan underneath, and cook for thirty minutes; reduce the heat to 325 degrees and cook another thirty minutes, according to the size of the bird.

The skin, which is by now a rich dark, shining brown, should be carved into one-and-a-half-inch squares, and served on a separate plate, or arranged to make an ornamental contrast to the meat, which should also be served in bite-sized pieces.

Both the skin and the meat are eaten with the warmed pancakes in the same manner as *mu-shi* pork, first placing some duck sauce on the pancake, laying across it some tasseled scallions, and wrapping up the skin or meat in its tube of pancake, and savoring the result.

As an afterthought, it would be well to prepare two ducks— they tend to disappear quickly. One duck will satisfy four people, and possibly six, but it is safer to have one in reserve.

A Szechwan way of preparing duck, which illustrates the relative mildness of Szechwanese banquet specialties, is the following. Although Szechwan peppercorns are used, they do not give the meat a strong, peppery flavor.

SMOKED TEA DUCK
CHANG CH'A YA

1 duck, about 5 pounds,
   preferably fresh-killed
2 gallons cold water
6 pieces five-star anise
1 tablespoon Szechwan
   peppercorns
6 fresh scallions
6 slices ginger root

1 teaspoon saltpeter
1 tablespoon salt
4 tablespoons wet jasmine
   tea leaves
vegetable oil, preferably
   cottonseed, for deep-
   frying

Cut off the tail with the oil sacs and wash the duck clean. Combine in a pot the water, anise, peppercorns, scallions, ginger root, saltpeter and salt. Bring to the boil, and boil for about fifteen minutes; then cool until lukewarm. Submerge the duck in the lukewarm mixture for about thirty-six hours. Turn every twelve hours to ensure that the bird is thoroughly marinated. Place the duck in a smoke oven over briquettes covered with the wet jasmine tea leaves for thirty minutes; then remove and steam in a bamboo steamer for about one and a half hours. Hang up to cool and allow the excess grease to drain off. (At this stage, the duck can be kept in a refrigerator for at least a week.) When ready to serve, split the duck in half, and deep-fry in vegetable oil until the skin turns a dark-brown color. Using a sharp knife or cleaver, disjoint the thighs, legs and wings; then cut the remainder into one-inch squares. This recipe, sufficient for four servings, produces a most savory dish, which, served near the beginning of a meal, is certain to awaken the taste buds and stimulate the appetite.

FIFTH MOON

After the relatively uneventful days of March, April and May, the fifth moon arrived with a bustle of activity and a coruscation of fireworks. It began with the Feast of Poisonous Insects, and led up to the Dragon Boat Festival on the fifth day following the full moon. Many ancient customs attended the Feast of Poisonous Insects, designed to protect one, literally or symbolically, from toads, lizards, scorpions, centipedes and serpents, all of which were reckoned venomous. A yellow spot of *hsiung-huang* (sulphur) was placed on our foreheads and around our nostrils and ears; and as a further safeguard and deterrent, my mother embroidered shoes for us with tigers on them, the head at the toe and the tail curling around the heel; and above these our ensemble was topped off with a yellow robe embroidered in black, to suggest the animal's stripes.

All night long sulphur incense burned, to discourage the evil insects, and in the daytime we waved *ch'ang-p'u* grasses, shaped like sword blades, to chase them away, in symbolic representation of Ch'ung-kuei, who can kill all devils. *Ai*, or wormwood, smelling strangely, was also used as a traditional insect repellent; and as an extra protection against some insidious attack, the young children had their heads shaved.

With poisonous insects satisfactorily disposed of, we could enjoy the unrestricted gaiety of the Dragon Boat Festival, which commemorates the search for the body of the upright minister of state Ch'ü Yüan (332–295 B.C.), who was degraded and dismissed from office for giving honest, if unpalatable, advice to his sovereign. Ch'ü Yüan thereupon committed suicide in the river which flows into the southeast side of the Tung-t'ing Lake in the province of Honan, to become forever in the eyes of his countrymen the model of the incorruptible statesman.

Brilliant streamers of silk and paper in cinnabar red and other bright colors dazzled in the sun; and the search for Ch'ü Yüan's body was re-enacted in Nanghai at a regatta, rowed on the middle reaches of the south lake in the Forbidden City, in which the beflagged boats, manned by young oarsmen, were enthusiastically cheered by the crowds watching them from the banks, to the sputtering and crackling of fireworks. Even if some overenthusiastic rower fell in, or an entire boatload was swamped, it only added to the excitement, and was certainly in keeping with the tragic event the festival set out to commemorate.

As always, special foods marked the occasion. It was mandatory to have *tsung-tzu*, glutinous rice cakes. In Canton they were about four inches long, two inches wide and an inch thick, but in Peking, shaped into a triangle. Both versions were intricately wrapped in the leaves of the lotus, or certain kinds of reed, and tied with natural black tendrils. The two principal kinds were the sweet and the salty, the salty being often filled with ham, or in Canton especially, with salty eggs. When the wrappings were unwound, the shiny semitransparent golden grains presented a distinct eating problem because they stuck to everything—the chopsticks, the fingers, and around the mouth. I never liked very sweet confectionery or dishes, which are not, in any event, characteristic of northern China as a whole, and therefore preferred the ham-filled cakes to the sugary kind, which had lotus seeds or fruits inside.

Since it was now both warm and humid, the customary shaking-out of the winter furs took place, and the maids thereafter hung them inside-out in a windy spot away from the sun. We thankfully exchanged our quilted cottons and fur-lined garments for light, summery cottons, some as fine as georgette, for wearing at home, or the thinnest, purest silk, of a quality and fineness that never wrinkled, if we were going out on some special occasion.

Being a time of festival, the fifth moon is a favorite month for relatives to visit without warning, making it imperative always to have plenty of provisions on hand. This presented no difficulty in our household, in view of my mother's careful husbandry and housekeeping; and our property at Ch'ang-hsin Tien, with its wide lands, provided an ample supply of fresh vegetables. When we went there, on Saturday afternoons after school, we always liked to pick the small, green, unripe apricots, of a sourness that sets my teeth on edge at the memory, and then eat them after dipping them in a special kind of honey. The fruit had a large nut inside, which we opened to extract the white kernel, and this, in turn, we rubbed until it was quite lustrous—to keep, in the way children often do, as a treasure.

When our relations called unexpectedly, there might also be some entertainment, since my Number One, Two and Three sisters all sang classical Chinese opera, and my Number Three sister had a particularly good voice. It was she who lived at T'ang-shan, a famous mining town not far from Peking, and whose *amah*, hump-backed and hideous, lived with her all her life, dying eventually in her service at about the age of ninety.

My Number One sister was always considered the beauty

of the family, tall, with classic features. She long retained her looks, and I recollect that years later, in Shanghai, just after she had succeeded in getting out of Peking in 1949, when she was over fifty and no longer used make-up, friends would ask me who that beautiful woman was. With the combination of her voice and loveliness, she was nicknamed "Mei Lan Fang," after the famous actor of feminine roles on the Peking stage.

Mei Lan-fang was certainly, in living memory, the greatest interpreter of the female roles in Chinese opera. Although he had an exceptionally high voice, it was never "pinched," and he combined a most beautiful face with exceptional grace of movement and gesture. The Chinese actor has to perform on short stilts in these parts, in order to suggest the swaying gait of the women with bound feet, and Mei Lan-fang's exquisitely poised motion completely conveyed the illusion. He was sixty-three years of age when I first met him, and we dined together in Shanghai on V-J Day, and went afterwards to the theatre. I complimented him on his youthful looks, and he smiled and replied, pointing with an expressive gesture to his head, "Oh, no! I am old—see, I have three gray hairs!"

The play that evening, *Ch'u Hai T'ang*, told the story of a young woman, played by a young actor I also knew, who was being persecuted by a brutal warlord. I was touched to see that Mei Lan-fang wept at the young actor's performance, and he told me that it reminded him of a tragic episode in his own life, when he had been similarly ill-treated. An unhappy sequel to the story is that the actor who had shown such talent that evening and whom we visited with congratulations after the play had ended, was later done to death by extremists.

The Chinese theatre, possibly because acting is confined to male performers, has a certain equivocal reputation, and Mei Lan-fang did not escape suspicion in this regard. As he eventually married twice, and had a son and a daughter, he was no longer looked upon in that light; certainly the Chinese as a whole are a normal, well-balanced people, possibly because of their closely structured family life, and the acting profession, which is set apart from the community, is almost alone in developing homosexual tendencies.

Mei Lan-fang played only in what would be called, in Occidental terms, grand opera, Ching-hsi, or "opera of the capital," Peking, such as my sisters sang. In those days, in the twenties and thirties, it was still fashionable to sing in this style, and it is very beautiful when well done. When my sisters performed, my father would sometimes accompany them on his *hu-ch'in*, a three-stringed violin, or on another of the classical instruments. He also liked the southern style, or K'un-ch'ü, which was slightly looked down upon in the north, although my father said it was equally difficult to sing. The chief instrument supporting the voice was the cross flute (*ti*), which my father also played, as well as the one called *hsiao*, which was played vertically.

One interesting aspect of Chinese opera is that for each type of role there is a corresponding voice: whether the actor plays an old man, an old woman, a young man, a girl, a villain or a hero, he must change his mode of singing for each. The make-up, too, is elaborately stylized, and the actor has to learn how to reproduce the same facial pattern every time. A villain, for instance, is painted in schematic arrangements of red, black and white, to suggest a distorted, evil face, so that one knows, as soon as he comes upon the scene, exactly what he represents.

In ordinary life, the ladies of those days used little make-up, and what little there was came from simple preparations made at home. Eyebrow pencils were unknown: instead, wooden matches were charred and applied to make a fine curved line; and powder was in cake form, needing a brush to soften it into a usable state before it could be put on—and it was dead-white. Rouge and lip salves were both prepared from flower dyes and applied in liquid form, with water, and if Chinese women wanted to dye their hair, a black wash, made from crushed black seeds, was brushed through their tresses. To fix the hair in position, thin strips of a special kind of wood (*pao-hua*) were soaked in water to extract a gummy substance, which had much the same effect as a spray. Fortunately, all my family retain their hair color, and I never saw my mother use any dye on hers. As for permanent waving, it was completely unknown, as were creams and cosmetics, even to protect one in the bitter days of winter.

I did not take part in the musical diversions of my elders in my early youth, and after graduating from grammar to junior high school when I was about thirteen or fourteen, was much more interested in outdoor sports, or in learning to ride on a friend's bicycle in the vast schoolyard where we had our tennis and basketball courts. When I was reasonably proficient, my mother bought me a light French model with hand brakes, on which I rode to classes.

After six years at the Bridgeman Academy I went for four years to Fujen University, at Shih-ch'a Hai, near Pei Hai, which was thirty or forty minutes away by bicycle from my home. In college I acquired a more modern bicycle, with a foot brake, although with any kind it was a hard ride, hot in summer and cold in winter, pedaling against the wind from the Gobi Desert.

I explored, as I grew older, every nook and cranny of Peking, so that I came to know all the out-of-the-way alleys. One narrow street sold only furs; another was devoted exclusively to jade; still another had finely wrought metal; and in another one could find exquisite carved ivory and painted fans. One sinister area was T'ien Ch'iao, "Heaven's Bridge," the place of stolen goods. Hither people came before dawn, to see what could be found, exchanging hand signals with the merchants without removing their fingers from their horseshoe-cuffed sleeves. I believe most, if not all, of these picturesque lanes have been swept away, just as the little shops in Tokyo where one used to find delicate beads and thread, and many other wares, have almost completely disappeared.

There was still the month to be played out before the long summer vacation, and we had to expect an end-of-term examination, involving much memorizing of classical poems and texts. Fujen University is of interest to anyone with any knowledge of Chinese literature since it is believed to be on the site of the palace described in *The Dream of the Red Chamber*, the eighteenth-century novel which epitomizes the way of life and thought of the nobility of the Ch'ien-lung period; and which, because of its descriptions of unrequited and incompatible love, has been cried over ever since by generations of young Chinese girls.

Since we were always brought up to conceal our emotions, and were therefore, for the most part shy and unable to express our feelings openly, it was not unusual for girls to fall ill as the result of ill-assorted love affairs which had never ripened, and "love-sick" is a precise translation of the Chinese term. Young women often developed tuberculosis and died as a result of emotional frustration, for the complications of matchmaking would often break off relations between young people because of differences in birth or fortune. Chinese literature is full of situations in which husbands are separated from wives and lament their fate, and I remember one celebrated poem which describes how a young woman was left by her husband and took shelter in a cave: eighteen years later he returned and no longer recognized the young girl he had abandoned.

In addition to *The Dream of the Red Chamber*, we also

read, more furtively, the novel known as *Chin P'ing Mei*, which relates the betrothal of the three young women of the title, their marriages and love affairs. Our parents would certainly have disapproved if they had known, for it was always censored. It was explicit in its details of lovemaking, and was thus often surreptitiously introduced into the dowry chests of young brides, to give them some inkling of the married state (mothers were too prudish to explain anything to them in person). Chin, in the story, is very beautiful and dynamic, and marries a small man, with a tall, handsome brother who rejects her advances. P'ing is quite different—gentle and feminine and compliant. Mei, the third heroine, typifies the good housewife, looking after her home and her husband. Although nobody was supposed to have read it, the novel was often quoted in making comparisons with women in real life.

As the season wore on towards the sixth moon, corresponding to the Occidental July, we sometimes paid brief visits to Pei-tai Ho, a summer beach resort on the coast east of Peking, where my uncle, my father's brother, had a villa. In the city it was growing so hot, without air conditioning, that the servants used to fan us with hand fans during meals, although as the walls of our ancient town house were nearly three feet thick, we were cooler than most. I enjoyed visiting and meeting people, and always made good friends in and out of school; and was never at a loss for things to do because I was always ready to improvise. If we could not get everything we wanted, we would always make something instead.

When we were tempted by Christmas decorations seen in magazines sent to us by some of our cousins who were being educated abroad, in the United States or in Europe, we used to copy them; and when my uncle, Ambassador Sha, was at the embassy at Oslo, he also used to send us periodicals which l over enthusiastically. He had older sons and daugh- had been brought up in Norway, and younger children who had spent their early years in Norway and then had come back to high school in Peking.

Ambassador Sha's house adjoined ours, although it was not as large since it did not have the garden to one side with the guesthouse, but it was of the same depth; and because the families were on friendly terms, my parents made a moon gate through from our house to his. His wife was my mother's cousin, one of the few relatives surviving—almost all my mother's family had died at an early age from opium-smoking, not at all an unusual custom in those days. Ambassador Sha was therefore more strictly a cousin by marriage once removed. He was a meticulously neat, dapper man, almost invariably dressed in Western clothes, and on formal occasions in morning coat, striped trousers, gray waistcoat, cravat and top hat, an amazing sight to us, and one that never ceased to fascinate us.

I often used to accompany my mother when she slipped through the moon gate to see my cousin-aunt, who detested the cold and the short days of Norwegian winters as much as Norwegian food and customs, and therefore spent as much time in China as she could. My mother and she would sit gossiping and cracking melon seeds, which are flavored in all kinds of ways in Peking, and I would sit and watch. What riveted my attention was the strange behavior of my aunt. In one hand she held a mortar, covered with a fine silk handkerchief, tied around the rim with a string. Through a hole in the center of the silk protruded the handle of a pestle, and as she and my mother conversed, she ground away continuously. Curiosity at length compelled me to ask my mother what my aunt had been doing, and she explained that she was grinding pearls.

I discovered, finally, the whole strange story. My uncle and aunt were both inordinately anxious to retain their youth, and therefore regularly ate ginseng and pearls. The pearls, admittedly not of the finest water, shape or size, but mis-shapen, baroque little seeds, were believed to have the property of preserving and beautifying the skin, making it have the luster and beauty of a pearl itself; and strangely enough, both my uncle and his wife had oddly un-Chinese skins, abnormally white, with a rosy flush.

My aunt had previously confided the pounding operations to the maidservants, who were thought to be more painstaking than the men, but as the pearls were expensive, even when sold by the ounce, she took to weighing them and found she was being robbed. Part of the complex procedure was this rite of weighing after the pearls had been bought, to be sure that the merchant had given the right measure.

Of the eventual pearl dust my uncle consumed vast quantities, washed down with wine. And yet this beauty treatment killed him. My uncle developed a hardening of the arteries, the result, perhaps, of an excessive ingestion of calcium, which led to high blood pressure and death. "Look," my father said. "He always wanted to appear young and beautiful, and now see what has happened!" My father always liked a good life, but moderation was his watchword.

I continued to copy objects seen in magazines or in the movies, and drew pictures of Western shoes in order to have our shoemaker imitate them; and much later, when I lived in Chungking, after 1943, I attempted to have the shoemaker there do the same for me. Chungking, however, was not Peking: it was at least thirty years behind the times, and when I took my drawings to the shoemaker he protested he had never seen or made anything like these foreign objects; but I insisted I wanted them specially for a party, and stood over him and showed him how I wanted them to look, and he succeeded in the end.

My early training in making my own amusements has always helped me. If I see how something is done, I feel I can do it: the difficulty of doing it never enters my mind, as it seems to me that if you understand how, you can do anything you choose. In the same vein, although I do not know how to sew, I know exactly how to tell a dressmaker what I need, and I suspect, if I chose, I could very well do it myself.

INTERLUDE
Of an Elderly Relative
and Elegant Simplicity

O CCASIONS ARISE IN EVERY HOUSEHOLD when guests arrive, or elderly relatives, who should be entertained with some style, and yet far short of a banquet. My mother would naturally make protestations that a very simple meal was being prepared, and my relations would beg her to go to no trouble on their behalf, and both would have been equally surprised to be taken literally. Some pretense of family style would be made, in that the dishes would for the most part be served all at once, but the individual dishes were more choice.

My mother was noted for her way of preparing chicken with the sweet chestnuts from Tientsin, a red-cooked preparation known as *li-tzu hung-shao chi*, which was well suited to the occasion (after some introduction such as Chinese sausage, or an egg dish, such as I have described in the second interlude), and was possibly preceded by some nibbling of watermelon seeds and nuts.

For seafood, an elegant dish was *ch'in-ts'ai ch'ao hsia-jen*, an Oriental type of celery stir-fried with small shrimp, or *wan-tou ch'ao hsia-jen*, a combination of shrimp and tiny snow pea pods. The celery was carefully cut to pair up with the size of the shrimp and the snow peas, and the guests would appreciate this subtlety, and the luxury of the ingredients.

In contrast, we might expect *cha-ts'ai cheng chu-jou ping*, pickled vegetables, Szechwan-style, with steamed pork.

An extremely good vegetable dish, *hung-shao ch'ieh-tzu*, red-cooked eggplant cooked with scallions, lean pork, chicken stock, soy and a little wine, complemented the other dishes, although eggplant was chiefly associated with the celebration of the Double Seven, the seventh day of the seventh moon.

Reinforced with the eggs, bean curd, bacon and ham from our stores, the menu provided a simple dinner, which nevertheless would maintain my mother's reputation as a hostess of taste. And there was still the soup: a refreshing combination of fresh bean curd and spinach in chicken stock.

RED-COOKED CHICKEN WITH CHESTNUTS
LI-TZU HUNG-SHAO CHI

1 fresh frying chicken, 3 pounds	1 whole scallion
¼ pound fresh chestnuts	4 tablespoons dark soy sauce (Japanese Kikkoman or Chinese imported)
1 large piece fresh ginger root, 3½ inches long	1 tablespoon sugar (scant)

This dish is always made with the meat still on the bone. After washing and cleaning the bird, cut off the head; retain the neck if this part is liked. Cut the chicken in half, lengthwise, and sever into pieces about one and a half inches in length, cutting cleanly with a heavy cleaver at right angles to the bones (it is always most important not to crush chicken bones, as they easily splinter). You should now have about twelve equal-sized pieces of chicken, with the skin still attached. Put the chicken pieces into a pot, cover with cold water, and turn the heat to high. In a separate *wok* or pot put the chestnuts to boil in plenty of water for ten minutes, then pour off the water, remove the shells and skins, and cut any large ones in half. When the water in which the chicken pieces are cooking boils, remove the scum, and at this stage see that the pieces are well covered with liquid—add some chicken stock if necessary. Put in the chestnuts, the ginger root and the scallion, cover, reduce the heat to a simmer, and cook for fifteen minutes. Since you want to end up with only a modicum of reduced sauce, pour off some of the broth, which can be kept for stock. Remove the lid and add the soy sauce. Then turn the heat high and shake the pot vigorously and repeatedly, for the liquid as it reduces may make the chicken stick, and you also want to distribute the red color of the soy evenly over the chicken and chestnuts. When the liquid is reduced, add the sugar and continue to shake for a minute or so to prevent the sugar from burning. When the dish is done, remove the ginger and scallion, and serve on a plate. (It was always regarded as a solecism to leave ginger or scallions in dishes in which they figured only as adjuncts to the seasoning.) This rich red preparation has a flavor and texture well suited to its brave color, which its slow reduction distills and concentrates.

The recipe is capable of a great many variations. You can, if you wish, use only half a chicken, and it is not necessary to cut it up if you are not going to use chopsticks. You can also combine the chicken with black mushrooms to produce an entirely different taste and "match"; or cook pork instead of chicken—only increase the cooking time to about one hour. Duck is also good red-cooked in this way. Beef takes much longer, about two hours for two pounds of beef. Spareribs are also very tasty, and the cooking time is about one hour. Once the method is mastered, the theme may develop its variations.

STEAMED PORK WITH SZECHWAN PRESERVED VEGETABLES

CHA-TS'AI CHENG CHU-JOU PING

¼ pound pork, with some
    marbling of fat
1 tablespoon chopped
    water chestnuts
pinch of salt
2 to 3 slices crushed and

chopped fresh ginger root
½ tablespoon Chinese rice
    wine
1 tablespoon water
5 slices Szechwan preserved
    vegetables (*cha-ts'ai*)

Chop the pork, not too finely, and mix with the water chestnuts, salt, ginger, wine and water. Slice the *cha-ts'ai* about one eighth of an inch thick, and put the slices on top of the meat mixture. Put the bowl in a preheated bamboo steamer, covered, for half an hour. The result is a piquant, highly flavored dish. A pleasant variation is to put eggs on the meat, producing a dish of poached eggs on steamed pork; or use salty eggs, which can be obtained from a Chinese grocery store.

SHRIMP AND SNOW PEAS

WAN-TOU CH'AO HSIA-JEN

½ pound large raw shrimp
    or prawns
1 cup cornstarch mixed
    with 1 cup water
4 ounces snow peas

2 tablespoons vegetable oil
1 tablespoon Chinese rice
    wine or dry sherry
pinch of salt

Shell and devein the shrimp, and coat lightly with the cornstarch-and-water solution. Prepare the snow peas by picking off both ends and removing the stringy fiber. Heat a *wok* over high heat and put in the oil, making sure that the surface is covered with a film of oil everywhere. When it is hot, put in the shrimp, and while rapidly stir-frying, add the wine and salt. Add the snow peas last, as they cook very rapidly, and in one minute, or less, all will be done. Speed and dexterity are essential in a dish of this kind, in which the elements are so fragile that overcooking will produce a tasteless, amorphous mess instead of a delicacy for the gourmet.

RED-COOKED EGGPLANT
HUNG-SHAO CH'IEH-TZU

1 eggplant, medium-sized
cottonseed oil
3 scallions (green part
    only)
¼ pound lean raw pork
½ teaspoon salt

1 cup chicken stock (see
    page 49)
1 teaspoon soy sauce
1½ teaspoons cornstarch
1 tablespoon Chinese rice
    wine or dry sherry

Cut the eggplant in quarters, lengthwise, and cut each quarter into four wedges. Soak the wedges for a few minutes in cold water (which turns black). Drain and deep-fry in very hot oil for about two minutes; set aside. Cut the scallions into two-inch sections. Stir-fry the pork in a small quantity of hot oil for about two minutes, then add the scallions, salt, chicken stock and soy sauce. Put in the wedges of eggplant and toss for about two minutes more, add the cornstarch (blended thoroughly with a little water) and the rice wine. Toss and stir for a few minutes more, until the sauce thickens, and then serve. This is a luscious, unctuous preparation and is cooked differently from nearly all other Chinese vegetables, which are almost invariably stir-fried rapidly without soy sauce. Eggplant can equally well be steamed, which also puts it in a class apart.

119

SIXTH MOON

JULY, IN PEKING, the time of the Lotus Moon, was a dormant month, when the heat induced lassitude, and the appetite faltered. The pulse of the whole city seemed to slow down; and our house itself, the windows and open corridors of which were shielded by semitransparent blinds of fine straw, the same fine woven straw that protected our bedding and all the furniture, appeared to be closing its eyes and withdrawing from the relentless sunlight.

If we ventured out in the middle of the day, shaded by parasols, we would pass by motionless bodies, topped by conical straw hats, huddled under the lee of a building, rickshaw boys seeking some respite from the heat. Everyone used a fan in an attempt to keep cool; the men carried the folding kind, tucked into their belts when not in use, and wore a more conventionally shaped straw hat as protection.

My mother always tried to persuade us, when we were young, to take a nap in the heat of the afternoon, but the sultry weather made us fidgety and restless, and we wanted to play, even at the expense of being uncomfortably hot. We drank hot tea at all hours of the day, and like the Japanese, had hot baths at this season, to cool ourselves by the simple process of evaporation. The best part of the day was after dinner, when we all sat in the courtyards, or in the garden pavilion (*pa-chiao t'ing*) to "catch the evening breeze" (*ch'en-*

liang), while our elders recounted old legends, recited poetry, or extemporized verses.

As a strict Buddhist, my mother would have liked us all to fast the entire month on a diet of vegetables. She herself punctiliously observed the rule of consuming no eggs, meat, fish, or any living thing at this time, not even wine, although she came to realize, reluctantly, that one cannot expect young children to be nourished on such a limited regimen, especially when we were on vacation from school and bursting with released energy. As for my father, as master in his own house and far from religious, he ate precisely what he liked; and if he chose occasionally to eat vegetables, it was simply because he considered it beneficial to give his body a rest in the hot weather, and eat lightly. As for us children, one of the few punishments handed out to us when we were young was to be forbidden a meal, and whenever this dire fate befell us, it was not effective in practice, as our *amahs*, naturally disposed to spoil us, would always surreptitiously slip food into our rooms.

Naturally, this lenten season put an end to banquets and parties, and we seldom entertained, and then only in a small way, until it had gone by; and because of that it would have been highly irregular and unusual to arrange marriages at this time since religious restrictions could not be waived and would have curtailed all the customary feasting and hospitality. This was also the closed season for the opera, and indeed, for almost all outside entertainment, so that one had to divert oneself at home.

I had started to ride on the sure-footed little northern ponies when I was about nineteen, after leaving high school, but it was too hot for this sort of exercise in high summer, and the ground was cruelly hard on one's mount. I used to ride on a track just outside the walls of the Legation Quarter, where there was a polo ground, and a kind of "Rotten Row" for equestrians. The Peking racetrack, unlike the one I came to know later in Shanghai, which was built in the center of the city by the British, lay outside the city walls, and was also closed until the cooler weather set in, and the first rains.

Another sound reason for not venturing much abroad was the unrelieved plague of flies and mosquitoes. It would have been pleasant, but for these, to have eaten sometimes out of doors: but as we used to chant when young, "There are so many mosquitoes, they could carry you." Nevertheless, Peking was not so much afflicted in this respect as some other parts of China. When I visited Hangchow in after years, I found an invading horde of mosquitoes in summertime, to say nothing of the appalling odors emanating from the many canals and waterways.

A few restaurants in Peking were set in gardens, or had roof gardens, and opened at sunset, but I did not come into much contact with nightclubs and night life until I lived in Shanghai or other more modern centers such as Tientsin. The first places ever to have air conditioning were the cinemas, and it proved so popular that a long break or intermission had to be introduced, for otherwise nobody could be persuaded to leave.

In spite of the sultry days—and nights—our mealtimes were as punctually observed as ever, except since we were on vacation and therefore joined our elders for tea and sweetmeats in the late afternoon, the dinner hour was retarded a little. In addition to hot tea, which in China was regarded as much more cooling than any cold drink, we refreshed ourselves between meals with imported grape juice and crab apple juice, poured over shaved ice, or with a concoction of red beans, cooked and ground to a paste (shells included) with brown sugar, and cooled likewise over shaved ice. We made ice cream as well, by the old-fashioned method, churned in a wooden barrel surrounded with freezing salt, and it tasted infinitely better than the commercial kinds of today.

Although the dishes at mealtimes were almost entirely vegetarian, they did not lack variety on that score. Our chief cook, inspired by my mother, who never lost interest in the kitchen however pious her religious observances, performed miracles of ingenuity in producing succulent and dissimilar repasts. Meats, fish, fowl, imaginatively concocted out of garden produce, continued to appear on our table.

Diversity was also achieved by cutting or carving radishes, scallions, lotus root, *yü-t'ou*, and turnip—the bright green sort which is a brilliant red within—into variegated flowers. One famous dish, *lo-han ts'ai*, or "the monk's dish," sometimes translated as the "Arhat's Fast," was made of from eight to twelve different vegetables, of which one essential component was the "hair" vegetable, a species of black seaweed brought from the south, resembling hair in appearance. The ingredients were usually all dried—tiger lilies, ginkgo nuts, mushrooms, peas, Chinese cabbage, bamboo shoots, bean curd, chestnuts—and it could be made most appetizing with the addition of oyster sauce. The vegetables always tasted crisp and inviting in these various preparations, as they were always rapidly cooked, and with rare exceptions, were never steamed or boiled or cooked with soy.

The most remarkable inventiveness, I think, was shown in the use made of bean curd. Some of it was pressed and dried in thin sheets, to become *tou-fu p'i*, "bean curd skin" (usually the kind included in the monk's dish), which was soaked in water, rolled up in tight layers spread with a little sesame oil in between, then tied with string and steamed, to emerge, finally, as *su huo-t'ui*, or "Buddha's ham"; after it was cooked, it was cut in slices, and looked uncommonly like rolled meat. Again, bean curd is found in tube form, as *fu-chu*, "bamboo bean curd." Dry-pressed bean curd, *tou-fu kan,* can be marinated, flavored, cooked in soy sauce and served cold, in slices. I remember eating fresh bean curd in Szechwan, which was delicious, and as it is generally low in calories and high in protein, it is especially useful at this time.

Associated in my mind with memories of the season is the eating of mashed green beans sprinkled with sugar, making a thick custard, *lü-tou kao,* which is sweet and refreshing. We also had *pai-ho,* a white root, shaped like garlic, boiled with sugar; candied lotus seeds were another favorite.

We enjoyed fresh fruits, of course, particularly watermelon, and melons in general; I liked most of all a small, crisp and sweet variety. In the absence of refrigerators, it was customary to place the fruit in a burlap sack, weighted down with stones, and lower them down the well, keeping them there until they were suitably chilled.

Pickled vegetables also featured largely on our table, prepared under my mother's eye, and Peking was famous for them under the name *ch'iang-ts'ai.* They were in keeping with the general custom in hot weather of avoiding anything oily or greasy, and were refreshing to the palate. Tiny, finger-sized turnips, cucumbers and baby corn ears, squash and all kinds of melon were first rapidly blanched in boiling water and then washed in cold. They were then dried by rubbing with a little salt, and finally pickled in soy, to which a little chili pepper was added. Special crocks were used for storage, shaped like flattened-down vases with narrow necks, covered outside with wickerwork, and inside, lined with heavy, oiled paper. The pot was sealed at the top and tied fancifully with string. I encountered a different method later, in Szechwan: *p'ao-ts'ai,* or "soaked vegetables," in which the ingredients were put into a deep jar with cold, boiled water, salt, Szechwan peppercorns (*hua-chiao*) and wine. All the vegetables in this method keep their original color. Apart from their appearance at breakfast, with congee, pickled vegetables were commonly served between courses at banquets, to nullify the flavor of one dish before beginning the next.

I am sure one does not have to be a Buddhist to benefit from eating thus lightly of garden produce during the hot weather; since in China there are usually good reasons behind traditional usage, a regard for health often enters into consideration in Chinese cuisine. Certain foods are regarded as "cold" for the body, and others as "hot"; and a balance by means of contrasted hot or cold spices or garnishes is characteristic. Pursuing this theory, we never ate "hot" lamb in summertime, only in winter, and on rare occasions, on cold days in spring. Herbs and fruits, as well as vegetables, fowl and fish, were thought of as "cold" or "hot," according to their nature, and I myself have suffered from nosebleeds which I attributed to eating too many "hot" lichee nuts.

In winter, when windows were sealed up with paper and stoves heaped with coal overnight, the air became too dry, causing sore throats and irritated noses, and consequently one was given "cold" turnips and pears, which were considered beneficial. The hot and cold principal also applied to indigestion. If some food disagreed with one, the saying was, "It brings the fire up," or *shang-huo*, and for this reason, hot dishes were always matched with cold elements, as though introducing the reciprocals of *yin-yang*, the balance, or complementary use of opposites. If, for instance, one ate a great deal of crab, as was the custom in autumn, it was always eaten with a sauce of "hot" ginger, brown sugar and vinegar, and wine was drunk with it. Crab and cucumber were never served together, as in the West, as both were classified as "cold"; and eggplant comes under the same heading, and is therefore usually prepared with ginger, for contrast.

Some foods were believed to be generally preservative of health and life, such as ginseng, bird's nest, white wood-ear and *wu-la ts'ao* which last my mother used to procure at great expense from Manchuria (whence also came mink, to line her clothes), and which the maidservants would clean patiently with tweezers to remove any impurities, just as they did with the bird's nest, picking out any tiny remnants of feathers.

Medicines were usually in powder form, and herb treatments were used even for broken bones and internal injuries. In the absence of any Occidental pills or vitamins, rest was regarded as the best cure for everything, supplemented by the traditional family remedies handed down in each household. From Yunnan came an especially potent white powder, *pai-yao*, which was contained in a small bottle and regarded as a sovereign specific for internal injuries of whatever kind; mixed with water it could be applied externally. A renowned Peking remedy was *kao-yao*, a thick, gluey substance wrapped up in the middle of a square of rice paper. When unfolded, it could be bound against the affected part, like a poultice.

I never heard of anyone submitting to surgery in those days, although no doubt it was often needed, and probably many people died from what were then regarded as natural causes when they might have been saved with more sophisticated techniques and treatment. Tuberculosis was the commonest disease, and many of my relatives were victims. Nothing was known of the way it was spread, so that one child in a crowded classroom might infect many; and in close family circles the risk of contagion was equally high.

Measles was successfully treated by shading the windows and lamps with red cloth to avoid injury to the eyesight, a common aftermath of the disease, and keeping the patient on a light diet of congee and pickled vegetables and a quantity of fluids.

If one child caught an infection, it was thought best for any others in the household to have it and get it over with—that is, if it was a childish complaint. Thus, when my daughter

129

developed measles in Tokyo, my son was put in the same room so that he would contract it as well, fortunately without serious consequences to either. Malaria was also common, owing to the lack of precautions taken against mosquitoes. Although I successfully avoided this and most other serious diseases, I did succumb to typhus, the dangerous spotted kind, which I caught in Chungking. The Chinese treatment was remarkably successful, concentrating on a light diet and complete avoidance of spicy foods, which would have irritated the stomach and thus indirectly aggravated the incidence of the spots.

I think most young children were glad when the sixth moon had passed because there was so little to do. Of course Peking was full of historic monuments, innumerable shrines, temples, lamaseries and mosques, served by Buddhist priests and nuns, Tibetan lamas and even Mohammedans, but I was always frightened by the uniformly dark and dirty interiors, lighted by small, guttering candles, with mud floors that struck a chill into one's bones even in summer, and were bitterly cold in winter. They have instilled in me a permanent dislike of guided tours and "places of interest," at which information drones out from ill-informed guides, with the day ending in fatigue, boredom and headache.

If the days of the sixth moon were spent in my childhood in an atmosphere of calm and relaxation, in which only the flies and mosquitoes came to disturb the halcyon summer, this picture of July in Peking was rudely shattered one hot night in 1937, the ill-omened Double-Seven, the seventh of July by the Western calendar, when the Japanese incident at the Marco Polo Bridge startled the world. We were peacefully sleeping when the noise of gunfire awakened us. We were thoroughly terrified and hid under our beds, as we had no idea what had happened, and it was not until the next day that we heard the news on the radio, and at high school, in the morning, we were told of the invasion. After this we could never go to Ch'ang-hsin Tien any more.

Hatred for the Japanese had been building up for many years: the markets of China were flooded with Japanese merchandise, to the exclusion of Chinese products, and as a result the city was plastered with posters with such slogans as, "Down with Japanese Imperialism," "Boycott Japanese Goods," and the persistent infiltration was watched with growing anger and frustration.

The coming of the Japanese was a turning point in our lives. From this time onwards truckloads of Japanese soldiers streamed into the capital, since Peking was used for the Japanese soldiers on leave. Japanese bars and restaurants, off limits to the Chinese, sprang up everywhere, and the Imperial troops, short, tough and ugly, came ever closer. I was astonished to see that girls always came with the troops, without understanding the reason. The Japanese, with a high regard for the practical, maintained the high morale of their fighting men by providing them with feminine company wherever they went. Geisha houses were set up throughout the city, and the best of food was allocated to the men. We were soon reduced to eating rice husks; and the disagreeable intimidation of every household began. Japanese officials started to come to our house to check for any subversive activities. Our servants were so frightened that they became speechless and stood with their teeth chattering and limbs trembling. I was remarkably fearless then, and often had the task of showing them around the house. There was no pretense of the much-vaunted Japanese politeness; they were uniformly rude, arrogant and boorish. The chief concern of these officials was to uncover food hoarding, to look for proscribed printed material, weapons, pistols, bombs. When they thumbed through books and did not find what they were looking for, they threw them contemptuously on the floor.

The next few years were to become increasingly unpleasant, as the grip of the occupying forces grew stronger and more confident. Japanese was made a compulsory study in schools, but however much I disliked it, it was later to prove useful.

INTERLUDE
Of the Mandarin Way
with Vegetables

THERE WAS NO HARDSHIP INVOLVED in eating vegetables to the exclusion of all other foods twice a month, according to Buddhist rule, or for the whole period of the sixth moon, because China was so rich in produce of that kind. And although the harvest of vegetables was seasonal, it was still varied enough to present no problem for the imaginative cook, especially in combination with bean curd, which is astonishingly adaptable at transforming itself, metamorphosing at the whim of the chef into the guise of rolled meat or chicken.

Even banquets were prepared, as I have explained, consisting purely of vegetables, and I have no difficulty in recalling innumerable dishes my mother prepared at the prescribed time. She found it necessary to use separate *wok* and pots, as all the foods had to be prepared with vegetable oils and would have been ritually contaminated by the kitchen utensils used for our regular meals.

Among the simpler cold dishes to choose from at a banquet were some of great delicacy and refinement, although, as usual, they needed some preparation, and skillful handling if they were to be perfect. The following is an example.

THOUSAND-YEAR EGGS WITH BEAN CURD
P'I-TAN PAN TOU-FU

2 thousand-year eggs
4 pieces of fresh bean curd
1 teaspoon sesame seed oil
½ teaspoon soy sauce
pinch of sugar

dash of pepper
pinch of salt
a few leaves of coriander
finely chopped

The bean curd should be carefully cut into dice-sized cubes and the thousand-year eggs cut to match. You then toss both of these in the dressing of sesame seed oil, soy sauce, sugar, pepper, salt and coriander. The bean curd, being very delicate, must be handled carefully, or it will break up.

The banquet followed the set pattern of all banquets, and therefore could begin with various nuts, and proceed to an elaborate cold plate, imitating, in various kinds of bean curd, birds, beasts and flowers.

I have mentioned elsewhere the ingenuity with which bean curd "skins," *tou-fu*, could be rolled, and transformed into a semblance of meat. Prepared in the same way, bean curd can also be shaped to resemble a chicken drumstick, and then becomes "Buddha's chicken"—*su-chi.*

It may seem irregular that I mention thousand-year eggs as part of the menu, and it is true that in earlier times eggs were forbidden, but in my time they were admitted to the Buddhist rule. No such license was permitted in regard to broth for soup, which could not be made from chicken and depended on water as the basis.

Pursuing our vegetable banquet, we might select next *hung-shao tung-ku*, red-cooked black mushrooms, and in contrast, follow them with *tung-sun ch'ao hsien-ts'ai*, winter bamboo shoots with pickled mustard. Mustard is also known as *hsüeh-li hung*, or "red berry in snow," from its appearance when growing; and winter bamboo shoots are always considered the best. We also speak of spring and summer bamboo shoots (*ch'un sun* and *mao-sun*, respectively) and the kind known as *yüan-pao sun*, or "gold-pieces bamboo shoot," from its curved shape, which resembles the sword-like gold and silver currency of old China.

Oyster sauce bean curd, *hao-yu tou-fu*, marks the re-entry of bean curd in another disguise, contrasted with spinach and glass noodles, a simple and delicate dish to prepare, or alternatively, chopped spinach with shredded bean curd, equally light and attractive.

SPINACH WITH GLASS NOODLES

PAI-TS' AI CH'AO FAN-TZU

⅛ pound glass noodles	1 teaspoon salt
1 pound spinach	pinch of sugar
2–3 tablespoons cottonseed	pinch of cornstarch
or peanut oil	dash of soy sauce (optional)

Soak the noodles in hot water for one hour (alternatively, they can be put into boiling water for two or three minutes before beginning the preparation); then drain and rinse them well in cold water to prevent their sticking together, and drain once more. Wash the spinach in plenty of cold water to remove the grit and cut off the ends of the stems, leaving the red part at the base of the leaves for an attractive color note. Now heat the oil to bubbling in a *wok* or deep skillet; add the salt and then the spinach and stir-fry (*ch'ao*) for about one minute. Next, continuing to stir rapidly, add the noodles, the sugar and the cornstarch (mixed smoothly with a little water), and stir-fry quickly to blend all the ingredients. A little sprinkling of soy sauce may be added according to taste.

CHOPPED SPINACH WITH SHREDDED BEAN CURD
PO-TS'AI PAN TOU-FU KAN

1 pound spinach	2 or 3 drops sesame seed oil
dry pressed bean curd	pinch of sugar
dash of soy sauce	1 or 2 drops Chinese vinegar

Wash the spinach thoroughly to remove all traces of grit, and cut off the ends of the stems, leaving the red part at the base of the leaves. Boil in a little water for two to three minutes. Mince the spinach and an equal quantity of dry pressed bean curd. Put into a bowl and toss with the soy sauce, sesame seed oil, sugar and vinegar, and serve cold.

Mushrooms of many kinds are employed in these vegetarian meals, such as the delicious straw mushrooms, small and delicate; button mushrooms; black mushrooms, either alone or in combination. Chinese long string beans can be matched with black mushrooms, which are sliced in strips to approximate the shape of the beans. They taste good when they are quickly *ch'ao*-cooked in vegetable oil with a little soy sauce and a pinch each of salt and sugar.

Since wine formed no part of a Buddhist banquet, one had to depend on the soup for drink, unless one had fruit juices; and black mushrooms might well figure again, in combination with winter melon, as *tung-kua tung-ku t'ang*, the banquet's soup.

Ginkgo nuts with Chinese cabbage is another dish which has an original flavor and texture; and eggplant, red-cooked or steamed, provided a change of pace. Sweet-sour green peppers and celery were other candidates at our banquet.

Towards the end of the feast, for such feasts do come to an end, there might be served *su chiao-tzu*, steamed vegetable dumplings, filled with wooden ear and hard-boiled eggs, or with eggs sautéed with vegetables and then steamed. *Chiao-*

tzu were also used as a dessert mouthful, stuffed with sweet bean paste or Chinese red dates. Desserts were quite varied, even with the restrictions, and such preparations as *lü-tou kao*, a kind of green bean custard blended with sugar, or silver ear (sometimes called cloud ear) prepared equally with sugar, taro root in a sweet *kuei-hua*–flavored syrup, walnut tea, and an almond float made with agar-agar, indicate the possibilities.

SEVENTH MOON

It has always surprised me that the day for lovers in the Western world is commemorated in the unsympathetic month of February, often the most bitterly cold of the entire winter. In China it always falls within the span of high summer, on the day of Double Seven, when magpies make a bridge across the heavens to enable Niu-lang, the herdsman, to meet Chih-nu, the spinning maid—a legend that would surely lose much of its romance if they had to meet in the night sky muffled up in fur coats.

The tale must be of extremely ancient origin, looking back, I suppose, to early astrological beliefs, since Niu-lang personifies agriculture and corresponds to Altair, and Chih-nu personifies weaving, under the guise of Vega, and at this time of the year they are bright in the night sky. If it rained, we used to say it was the lovers weeping because they were separated. Although old customs in connection with this anniversary were kept up in rural areas—housewives and young women, for instance, prayed to Chih-nu to improve their sewing—we did not make any special occasion of it beyond recalling the romantic story and eating eggplant grilled with wheat flour very plainly in the northern style, with a lot of chives.

It was hotter than ever during the seventh moon, although the mood differed a little, since religious restrictions were lifted, even if one still preferred to eat simply and lightly while the heat continued. The whole city remained quiet and shielded from the sun, and within the confines of our house the gardeners cooled the courtyards by sprinkling the flagstones and the flowerbeds with brooms dipped in buckets of cold water: a singularly ineffectual method, for the steam rose at once from the ground as the drops evaporated, and the courtyards were soon as hot as before. (In Chungking, where I lived in after years, the air was heavy with moisture from the mist known as *chang-ch'i*, which was trapped in the gorges where no breath of wind could reach to blow it away. The walls of the houses appeared to sweat: one had to put strong lime, smelling like disinfectant, around the edge of every room to absorb the moisture.)

As the summer vacation went on its quiet way, we stayed in our closely knit family group; and it was an opportunity, had I thought then of considering it, of taking stock of our differences. Unlike my parents, all the children married late by Chinese standards, in their mid-twenties, or thereabouts. My eldest sister, the classic beauty, was married first, according to tradition—one was supposed to marry in strict order of seniority, so that the older girls would not lose face—and had many virtues: she was as intelligent as she was beautiful; she became a good cook, sewed exquisitely, and could compose poems. Number Two sister was a brilliant scholar, but her domestic skills were limited to housekeeping; she married a professor at Tsing Hua University, and like my Number One sister, went during the war to Yunnan, where her husband continued to teach at the University of Kunming. My third sister and her husband were devoted to Chinese opera, which she sang, as I have mentioned, exceptionally well, and my father was especially fond and proud of her for that reason. All three of the eldest girls were tall. My third sister

144

also had beauty, although not framed in the classical mold of the first.

My father played a little calligraphic joke in naming my Number Four and Five sisters. They were very small twins, bright and charming, and unusually good at all games, tennis, ice skating, and basketball. Number Four he named Ling and the other, the Fifth, was called Chin, the characters for their names being written respectively

The extra brushstroke at the bottom of Number Four's—the only difference between the two characters—recorded the little cyst, like a round pearl on one of her ears.

My Number Four sister wasted away and died during the Japanese occupation, either from lack of nourishment as a result of the severe rationing or possibly even from tuberculosis: if from tuberculosis, it was fortunate she had a room to herself and servants to look after her or the infection might have spread further around the family. Unlike the other *amahs*, my Number Four sister's *amah* had returned to her husband and borne another child, and then came back to our house to nurse me, and in so doing became my *amah* instead. She left us again when I grew up.

My Number Five sister and I had naturally a certain amount in common because we both loved all games and sports. She eventually left China and settled in America, marrying an Episcopalian minister. My Number Six sister, gentle and attractive, also went to the United States.

I have to confess, no doubt because of the uncertain war

years and the difficulties of communication, that I was married, contrary to all custom, ahead of two sisters senior to me. Oddly enough, although twelve of the thirteen children married, not one had the large family our parents had, at most two or three, and usually only one boy and one girl, a remarkable change from the record of the past.

The seventh moon was seasoned with a number of festivals, such as that of the Hungry Ghosts, or Magnolia Festival as it was known to the Buddhists. It was celebrated on the fifteenth day, when spirits who did not enjoy the consolation of ancestral worship and therefore tended to harbor malign thoughts, were pacified with propitiatory offerings of fish, eggs, pork, cabbage, rice, wine, and even money, all of which were considered appropriate. For the living, it was customary to eat eggplant tarts, and Buddhists made it an occasion for a meatless banquet.

Towards the moon's end, on the twenty-ninth day, is the Festival of the Earth Spirit, Ti-tsang Wang, or, as he may also be called, Ti-tsang P'u-sa. Children always enjoy his festival, for they are allowed to rush about planting bundles of smoldering incense sticks in front of every house. When Ti-tsang Wang opens his eyes on this day to look for any spirits who may have strayed from the Ti Yü (the Infernal Regions), he will smell the fragrance of the incense and find the world beautiful and acceptable. Ti-tsang Wang, the saviour-divinity, who can open the gates of hell and protect the afflicted, is also kindly disposed towards the unfortunate ones among the living, and gathers them into the Buddhist fold. As the Hungry Ghosts Festival continues through the thirtieth day, this amiable deity can shepherd them safely back to the nether regions. We used to make patterns with the incense sticks in the shape of propitious characters, to give him pleasure.

Occasionally we varied the simplicity of our summer existence by going to the open-air restaurants, the Pei-hai Kung-yüan, in the park with the lakes, or the Chung-shan Kung-yüan, all of which served banquet-style meals in the cool of the evening, and tea and cakes during the day; but often we felt inclined to have only some cold congee with pickles, because of the heat. We avoided pork or beef, and sometimes ate a little chicken, or a fish such as the *tai-yü*, which looked like a flat silver ribbon rippling in the water. It was prepared by red-cooking in a sweet-sour sauce made of vinegar, brown sugar, wine and a large quantity of ginger.

Fresh mint and sometimes white chrysanthemum petals were put into tea to cool and refresh one; and mint was also added to *lü-tou kao*, the custard made of green beans. Cucumber, the thin-skinned, seedless variety, was delicious when pounded with the flat side of a cleaver, chopped, and tossed with soy sauce and sesame seed oil, and radishes were treated in the same way, with the skin left on. I also liked cold noodles tossed with a dressing of soy, sesame seed oil, sesame seed paste, sliced cucumber, bean sprouts, slivers of ham and chicken, Chinese chives and a few dried shrimp to heighten the flavor.

The kitchen staff must have been relieved that we liked cold food at this time of the year. The kitchen had the worst location in the whole house, dark and stuffy and far from the main dining room: we needed a chain of servants to ensure food reaching the table hot. We ate simply, too, in summer. The noodles would be placed in a large bowl in the center of the table with four dishes around it all at once, unlike the separate procession of courses when we gave a party. In wintertime we also had special hot bowls with two compartments, one for food, the other for hot water; but these were not common, and most families depended more on the speed of their servants than the heat of the bowls. This question had raised special problems during the time of the Manchu rulers of the Ch'ing dynasty: they often chose to dine wherever they happened to be at any particular moment, and portable stoves had to be devised to enable the Imperial appetite to be assuaged without delay.

Tea was the great mainstay in quenching our thirst and helping us to keep cool. It is drunk in China with far less ceremony than in Japan, where the act of making it, and the way it is received, always seems more important than the tea itself. As far as ceremony is concerned, in China it is always offered when anyone comes to the house, and at their departure, and one offers and receives it with both hands, as a matter of etiquette. We drank it all day long, except at the dining table: a teapot never appeared at meals—only as an accompaniment to sweetmeats or snacks, which may come as a surprise to those accustomed to the ubiquitous teapot in Chinese restaurants in the West.

Ideally, it is better to prepare tea with water from a natural spring. Our family had a beautiful spring at Hui-ch'uan Shan, near Wu-hsi, which was excellent for making tea. In summer we preferred to drink green tea, *lü-ch'a*, often flavored with jasmine, and it could be quite expensive; the variety known as *hsiang-p'ien* might cost as much as five dollars a canister. Other summery teas were *lung-ch'ing* ("dragon well"), of which the best kinds are *yü-chien* ("before the rain"), made from the youngest and freshest leaves; *mao-chen* ("top of the shack"); and *yü-hou* ("after the rain"). *Pai-chü-hua ch'a*, chrysanthemum tea, using only the white-petaled variety, was thought to cool the blood.

The red teas (or "black" teas of Western terminology), *hung-ch'a*, were drunk mainly in the winter. One was *mei-kuei hung-ch'a* ("red rose") and another, *t'ieh Kuan-yin ch'a* ("iron Buddha"), also known as "cliff tea," which was grown in the mountains of Amoy and was believed to be harvested by agile monkeys. The very dark, digestive *p'u-erh*, was served at the end of banquets, to rinse the palate after the richness of bear's paw or shark fin: not served at the table, of course, but afterwards, in a separate room.

Steeped tea as it is drunk today is the method now favored by the Chinese, although I am told that the earliest way, employing brick tea, is still to be found in Outer Mongolia and parts of Russia. Whipped, or powdered tea, the method followed in the Japanese tea ceremony, originated during the twelfth century A.D. in the Sung dynasty. The Japanese copied this method of stirring the infusion with a whisk in hot water, and fossilized it in the elaborate ritual practiced today.

Much has been written about tea, and almost as much about the water required to prepare it: in the famous novel *The Dream of the Red Chamber*, a nun brews tea with snow water matured for three years, and shows her disdain when the vintage quality of the liquid is not fully appreciated. For me, tea should be a source of uncomplicated pleasure and not a pretext for a scholar's study; and this point of view has always made me a little impatient with the overrefinement of the tea ceremony, with its interminable protocol.

In our household we always followed these simple rules. Tea was always made in a porcelain teapot, which was heated with hot water. After the water had been poured away, the dry tea leaves were put in the pot according to one's taste. I think this is very much a matter of individual preference. We filled the teapot two-thirds full, and always poured the first cup back into the pot since it made the leaves sink to the bottom. We never used a large cup, always a small one of fine china; and some cups had lids, which were tipped slightly when one drank, to hold back the leaves: these were called *kai-wan ch'a*. Two rules were always respected. We never drank tea that had been kept overnight, which the Chinese believe to be injurious, and we never allowed the tea leaves to become dry at the bottom of the pot; hot water was always added before the tea had all been poured away.

I have sometimes regretted that I did not taste one rarity of the Chinese cuisine when I might have done so, but the palate of a child is sometimes fickle: thus I cannot claim ever to have tasted that great delicacy I have mentioned above, bear's paw, essentially a northern preparation requiring both time and skill. I have nevertheless enjoyed wildcat, whose meat is like chicken. It was prepared in chicken broth, with a number of "cold" herbs because it was considered "hot" for the body. It also formed one ingredient of a dish known as "dragon and tiger." Obviously, one cannot obtain dragons, and tigers are equally hard to come by, so the Chinese chef used to compromise with snake and wildcat cooked together: and I can testify that snakes, to my palate, taste even better than eels.

The sautéed eels of Wu-hsi were renowned. My mother used to have the eels flown in from her home city by plane. They were kept, dry and crisp, in a deep can with lime at the bottom: and they would eventually be cooked with some good ham in very hot oil with plenty of pepper, soy sauce and coriander. The Chinese eel is dark yellow, with a firm flesh, quite unlike the Japanese variety, which is black and tends to fall apart when cooked. Another most succulent method my mother used was to marinate and then deep-fry the eel. Wine was a good accompaniment too. My mother used to make a dressing of wine, vinegar, sugar and ginger finely chopped, or else put the pieces of eel into a clear broth of soup noodles. The oily sauce remaining from the first method was excellent for tossing with leftover foods—Chinese never like to waste good material. When I lived later in Japan I learned that Japanese men used to eat eels in the autumn, believing that they build up strength and virility—an opinion not shared by the Chinese.

Turtle was a delicacy prepared in a rather bloodthirsty way. The turtle was first fattened on rice until it was considered plump enough for the table, and it was then teased with a stick until it was enraged and poked its head out from the carapace to bite and seize hold of the tormentor. The chef then chopped its head off, drained away the blood and washed the turtle well. The meat was next chopped with the shell still attached to it, into chunks two inches square—the shell makes the broth—and it was cooked with a little wine and ginger to kill any fishy odor. There resulted a crystal-clear broth requiring no further seasoning: the original flavor was good enough.

We ate fish in the summer months more than at other times, since of course the rivers were frozen in winter and catching the fish presented extra difficulties. Fish were often served "butterflied" in our house, in Hangchow style, as in the preparation of *ts'u-liu yü*, which was poached in water, with the lid on the *wok*, together with a little soy, a lot of sliced ginger, and the shredded white parts of scallions. Vinegar was cooked with scallions, ginger, wine, a little starch and sugar, and the sauce was poured on top of the fish, to make a heavenly taste.

More accessible than the fish and eels from Wu-hsi were the very large prawns from Tientsin, of which the glutinous yellow part in the head was considered the choicest.

One delicacy common to China and Japan is the blowfish, which has to be prepared by specially licensed chefs because the poison sacs are lethal. There is a pithy Chinese saying, *Ning szu che hou t'uen,* "I'm ready to die; I'll try it." The flesh is white, and when it is served in paper-thin slices on porcelain it is quite transparent, and delicious. I have eaten it raw, in soup, and also with vegetables—and survived. The *tai* fish is also found in China, where it is usually steamed. It is like a goldfish in appearance but much bigger, and the Japanese slice the pinkish flesh, and then put it together again and serve it raw. In Shanghai, in the summer, the *shih-yü*, or shad, is popular; it has a lot of bones, and is wrapped in a caul of pork and steamed with ham, without removing the scales. The freshwater crab were also of unmatched flavor, but the time for eating them was later in the year, during the ninth moon.

All kinds of squash ripened during the seventh moon, and I especially remember an elongated variety which, when sliced, had the seed sections forming strange angles; it was more interesting to look at than to eat, being distinctly lacking in taste. On the other hand the *hsiang-kua* melon, like a honeydew in color, small, but long, I found only in Peking, and it was so crisp and juicy one could eat even the skin. The huge flat *shih-tzu* (persimmons) ripened at this time, and I recall the small white pears, *hsiao pai-li*, wrapped in rice paper and cotton, and kept until the winter.

Towards the end of the month we began to think of school, college, or university, depending on what stage we had reached; for it made very little difference as regards vacation time or studies. The Chinese curriculum had a rigid and solid succession of classes from eight in the morning until five in the afternoon, never varying throughout one's school days.

It was not until I left college that I learned to drive. I had a beau who had a Pontiac convertible, considered very dashing, and although the British Austin, the French Renault and the German Mercedes-Benz were popular, the American cars— for all automobiles were imported—were the most admired. I went on to continue my driving experience in a Cadillac convertible, owned by another friend, which was in the highest possible style, and I was thought "advanced" in consequence. Our family automobile was a Buick, and afterwards a Packard, upholstered in brown velvet, although the proprieties required that the outside be black. It was never large enough, of course, to hold the entire family, which was why we always went to Chang-hsin Tien by train, peering out of the windows for a glimpse of the Marco Polo Bridge, the landmark which showed we were nearing our destination.

There is so much variation in the lunar calendar in relation to the Western months that the seventh moon ended sometimes as late as the middle of the Occidental September, when the first chill of autumn had already set in; the days were shortening, and the evenings were clear and cool. Then we looked forward to the celebrations of our August Moon.

INTERLUDE

Some Thoughts on Desserts
and a Dinner
for a Distinguished Visitor

T HE READER MUST SURELY HAVE REMARKED BY NOW that desserts seem to play a singularly small role in Chinese eating, less, perhaps in northern China than most parts of the country, and they are certainly less sweet than those found in Canton. In the old days, sweet cakes and pastries were usually eaten between meals, with tea, and were sometimes accompanied by the more savory *chiao-tzu*, dumplings with meat or vegetable fillings. *Tien-hsin*, or "touch the heart" dainties, used to appear at *mah jong* parties, and today—as formerly —are eaten constantly between meals by the Cantonese, who call such snacks *dim sum*.

Desserts rarely appeared on our table in Peking except between courses at banquets, as a light diversion. Some were, however, almost *de rigueur* on certain occasions, such as a wedding feast, when Eight Precious rice, a pudding made from glutinous rice, appeared, steamed and stuffed with so many colored fruits and nuts that when it was turned out of its mold, a charming mosaic of colors emerged.

Most characteristic of northern sweet dishes were glacéed apples, bananas, or mountain yam (*shan-yao*), which are quite difficult to prepare single-handed, as at one critical point you have to do two things at once. Walnut syllabub (*ho-t'ao lao*)— we had walnut trees in one of the courtyards—was another: it is made from ground walnuts and preserved dates, with sugar and some condensed milk. Sometimes we had a purée of beans and dates: red beans, green beans and brown dates, arranged to display the three different colors. The beans were cooked so that the shucks could be easily removed, and they were then sautéed in peanut oil with a little sugar.

Fresh fruit, and of course the famous Peking preserved fruits, when the season provided no fresh ones, were the most frequently served. Fresh fruit often decorated a table at the beginning of a banquet, when nuts were nibbled at. Otherwise, fruit and nuts were eaten between meals, as *ch'ih chih war*, "eat for fun," and were, naturally, another choice for *mah jong* entertaining. I also recall a special Mohammedan milk dessert from Mongolia, called *nei ou-t'a*, obtainable only at the Tung-an Shih-ch'ang bazaar, where one could find almost anything. It was a little like yoghurt, and was sold out very quickly. Unless one looked for it in the early morning, it was soon all gone.

One much-touted dessert in modern Chinese cookbooks is Peking dust, a rich confection of roasted chestnuts, ground until they are like mashed potatoes, to which cream is added. The mixture is then put into a mold, with the whipped cream, and decorated with red dates and sometimes with a cherry on top. My mother knew nothing of this dessert in my early childhood, and it is said to have been invented by the Westerners living in the capital in the 1920's. The lavish use of cream certainly does not suggest an indigenous Chinese dish, although it might well have been invented by one of my ingenious countrymen who had noted the Occidental love of sweet, rich desserts. The chestnuts of Tientsin were sweet enough for Chinese tastes, but in the West, Peking dust is made with sugar.

Agar-agar, a gelatinous substance derived from seaweed, and resembling Jell-O, was mixed with egg and cornstarch, rolled in almonds or other ground nuts, and deep-fried. The result was a not too sweet dessert, like a fried custard, with a pleasantly crunchy crust.

The white (silver) wooden ear fungus, mixed with sugar—rock sugar was always used in my time for these preparations —and cooked slowly in water, was always regarded as a luxury and was reserved for banquets.

Glutinous rice was used in a number of ways, and I recall another Mohammedan sweetmeat, "fried lamb's tail" (*cha yang-wei*), made of glutinous-rice flour stuffed with bean paste and deep-fried. And the same sticky kind of rice was used for *nien kao*, in which the rice was mixed with brown sugar and a paste of dates, and then set in a wooden mold and steamed.

From desserts to cookies is a short step, and these varied greatly according to region and religion. Most Chinese used lard as shortening, whereas Mohammedans in the north made their cookies with sesame or peanut oil, goat's milk, or even goat fat! Sesame seeds were the most popular decorations, although peanuts and almonds were also used. It seems hardly necessary to add that fortune cookies, the invariable parting tidbits in a Chinese restaurant in the United States, were not to be found in China, and first saw the light in San Francisco.

Mandarin glacéed apples and bananas have such an element of the unexpected that they are well worth trying at a special party where the hostess, if not trying vulgarly to impress, at least wishes to extract a delighted reaction from her guests. We might compose a little menu for the occasion, a dinner, let us say, for the Distinguished Visitor, with Chinese dishes arranged into a Western menu:

Mandarin Chicken Salad
Chungking Beef
Szechwan Four Season Beans

One of the following:

Mandarin Glacéed Apples and Bananas
Eight Precious Rice
Walnut Syllabub

MANDARIN CHICKEN SALAD

PAN CHI-SSU

¼ of a fresh young
  3-pound fryer
3 or 4 thin slices fresh
  ginger root
2 or 3 chopped scallions
pinch of salt
¼ pound bean sprouts

SAUCE
2 teaspoons soy sauce
½ teaspoon sesame seed oil
1–2 teaspoons hot pepper oil
  (page 161)
½ teaspoon Chinese vinegar
shredded onion or 1 clove of
  garlic, chopped (optional)

Bone the quarter of chicken and poach gently in water to cover, with the ginger, scallions and salt. Cook until the meat turns white, remove from heat and allow to cool. Then tear the meat by hand into thin strips. Wash the bean sprouts carefully (if you wish to impress your guests with consummate elegance, trim the tail of each bean sprout—this is very time-consuming, and only the connoisseur might notice). Plunge them into boiling water for about five seconds, then immediately in and out of cold water. Drain well.

For the sauce mixture, the onion, in any quantity you please, should be finely shredded. The best way to prepare the garlic is to crush it with the flat side of a cleaver, and then chop it finely.

Mix the sauce thoroughly and toss the chicken and bean sprouts in it, and serve immediately. I have called this a salad, although the Chinese repertoire does not really have salads in

160

the Western sense: it is, perhaps, more accurately termed marinated chicken.

CHUNGKING BEEF
KAN-P'IEN NÜ-JOU

This is a spicy *ch'ao* dish, typical of northern China, where the ingredients are plentiful.

6 ounces lean beef
2 tablespoons cottonseed oil
2 medium-sized carrots
2 medium-sized stalks celery

1 tablespoon Chinese rice wine or dry sherry
dash of hot pepper oil (see below)
1 teaspoon soy sauce
3 drops fagara oil (see below)

To prepare the hot pepper oil, chop up with a cleaver or kitchen shears ¼ pound of red chili peppers. Heat 1 cup of cottonseed oil in a *wok* to 375 degrees. Add 4 whole scallions and a good-sized piece of ginger, whole and unpeeled, and turn off the heat immediately. After three or four minutes discard the scallions and ginger. Allow the oil to cool for about five minutes, then ladle it over the chilies in a cold steel bowl. Allow to stand overnight. Drain off the oil and bottle it. The chopped chilies remaining may be kept indefinitely in a covered jar under refrigeration, for use in cooking.

Fagara oil is prepared by the same method, using Szechwan peppercorns instead of the chilis. Both oils impart an inimitable flavor, for which there are no substitutes.

Slice the beef into thin strips, about ⅛ inch thick and about one inch by three in width and length. Slice the celery and carrots to match. Then heat a *wok*, put in the cottonseed oil, coating the sides thoroughly, and heat to 375 degrees. Add the strips of beef and stir-fry them well (eight to ten minutes).

They should be fairly well done and dry. Remove any surplus oil, then add the carrots, continuing to stir-fry rapidly for thirty seconds; then add the celery, rice wine, hot pepper oil, soy sauce and fagara oil. Stir-fry until the ingredients are well blended and the vegetables just barely tender; drain and serve. The resulting dish should be dry in character but fully flavored.

SZECHWAN FOUR SEASON BEANS
KAN-P'IEN SZU-CHI TOU

½ pound fresh, long green beans

3 tablespoons cottonseed oil

1 clove of garlic, minced

1 dozen finely chopped dried shrimp

1 tablespoon finely chopped mustard pickle

1 heaping tablespoon hot soy bean paste

1 tablespoon Chinese rice wine or dry sherry

1 teaspoon hot pepper oil (see page 161)

1 tablespoon soy sauce

1 teaspoon sugar

½ cup chicken stock (see page 49)

2 tablespoons cornstarch

Break the beans into two-inch segments. Heat a *wok* and put in the oil, coating the sides, and heat to 375 degrees. Add the garlic and cook for thirty seconds; then add the beans, dried shrimp, mustard pickle and hot soy bean paste, quickly stirring and tossing all the time. Add next the rice wine, hot pepper oil, soy sauce, sugar, chicken stock and the cornstarch (blended with water to make a smooth flowing paste). Continue to stir-fry rapidly. The timing depends on the reduction of the sauce, as the beans should, in the final result, be almost dry—and hot and spicy—and the sauce scarcely more than a glistening surface.

The pungency of this dish is, of course, typical of the province whence it comes, and is at its best in China in the summer, when the long string beans have their limited season.

MANDARIN GLACÉED APPLES AND BANANAS
PA-SZU P'ING-KUO HSIANG-CHIAO

3 semi-ripe bananas
2 Delicious apples
2 egg whites
1 tablespoon all-purpose
   flour

2 tablespoons cornstarch
cottonseed oil
3 tablespoons water
1 cup sugar

Peel and cut the bananas on the bias into four pieces each. Peel and core the apples and cut into one-inch cubes. Blend in a bowl the egg whites, flour and cornstarch, and add the fruit, making sure that each piece is completely covered with the batter. Next comes the crucial stage. You must have ready simultaneously, the oil heated to the bubbling stage (about 375 degrees) in a *wok* and close at hand, in another *wok* or pot, a syrup of the sugar and water which has been cooked until it forms a hard thread when a little is dropped in cold water (about 300 degrees on a candy thermometer; Chinese cooks of course do not use these mechanical aids). Put the fruit into the oil and deep-fry for thirty seconds or until a light golden brown. Using a Chinese strainer, transfer the fruit from the oil to the syrup, give a quick stir to ensure that the fruit is completely covered, and just as quickly transfer it to a large plate which has been thinly spread with cottonseed oil. Rush the fruit to the table, where you will have ready a large bowl of water in which ice cubes are floating. Under the astonished eyes of your guests, hastily put the syrup-covered fruit in the ice water, where the syrup will immediately harden to give each piece a crisp, candy-like shell, and serve. The thoughtful hostess will warn her guests that the fruit is still dangerously hot inside its cooler sugared coating, or the surprise will lose its charm. In all fairness, I think it would be wise to experiment a little, as the technique and speed required for this dessert needs a little practice, but once mastered it can be a dramatic climax to one's dinner party.

EIGHT PRECIOUS RICE

PA-PAO FAN

½ pound glutinous rice
preserved pineapple
preserved lotus seeds
preserved cherries
pine nuts
raisins

ginkgo nuts
watermelon seeds
sugar
1 can sweet red-bean paste
  (see page 21)
sugar-and-water glaze

Soak the glutinous rice for two hours in cold water. Then simmer in two cups of water until slightly soft, and then for fifteen minutes more. Sweeten according to taste. Cut the fruits into varied patterns and arrange in a decorative scheme on the bottom of a large bowl, six inches in diameter, and about three inches deep. Now put half the drained rice on top of the fruits, taking care not to disturb the pattern. Next add a layer, about one quarter of an inch deep, of the sweet red-bean paste, spreading it a little short of the sides of the bowl, and top off with the remainder of the rice. You may need a little more sugar, to taste, as the red-bean paste is not sweet enough for everyone. (If the pudding has been made in advance and kept in the refrigerator, it must be steamed for three hours before serving.)

To serve, reverse the bowl, holding it against a plate, and tap sharply to detach. If all goes well, the eight precious rice pudding emerges in all its colorful glory, with the fruits firmly embedded in their preordained design. Now glaze with a mixture of hot water and sugar, as the final touch. Spoon portions of the pudding onto individual plates, and try to preserve the decoration in its place.

WALNUT SYLLABUB
HO-T'AO LAU

I have called this a syllabub rather than a soup (as it is sometimes translated) because a hot liquid of nut purée, dates and sugar, with milk and a touch of cognac, hardly qualifies as a soup in Western terms, and the consistency should be that of a flowing custard.

½ pound walnuts
¼ pound preserved dates
1 tablespoon condensed milk

½ cup sugar (or more, to taste)
1 teaspoon cornstarch
1 tablespoon cognac

Shell the walnuts and remove the skins by soaking in hot water to cover for thirty minutes. Drain and then bring the walnuts to a boil in enough fresh water to cover, simmer for five or six minutes, and drain again.

Soak the dates for half an hour in two and half cups of cold water, then drain. Bring to a boil in four cups of fresh water, immediately reduce the heat, cover, and simmer for about half an hour. Allow to cool, drain, reserving the liquid, and remove the skins and kernels.

Put the date pulp and walnuts into a blender with a cup of

165

the date water and blend until smooth. Pour the purée into a saucepan and slowly stir in the condensed milk. Then add the remainder of the date water, about two cups of cold water, and the sugar, and simmer, bringing gradually to a boil, stirring constantly to prevent sticking or burning. Immediately reduce the heat to a simmer, add the cornstarch (blended with a little water), and cook until the syllabub begins to thicken. Add the cognac, and serve while hot. The syllabub should be served in bowls, and is eaten with a spoon.

All the stirring and mixing had to be done by hand in our household, as we did not know of the electric blender, and it is just possible that the results were better, since one controlled the preparation at each stage. The introduction of the cognac was an embellishment of my father's, and is certainly an improvement.

EIGHTH MOON

In many ways, late September and early October are the most beautiful time of the year in Peking: the sky is serene and clear, and the autumn leaves turn to russet and gold. The city comes alive again after the heat of summer; the opera reopens, and banquets and parties are planned for the Festival of the August Moon, Chung Ch'iu, on the fifteenth day. This was a particularly happy time for me when I was a child, for this was when Ch'ang-o, the beautiful Moon Lady, came down from the sky to give young ones their dearest wish. We would always receive a clay rabbit, dressed up as a high-ranking official—these rabbits were sold at street stalls everywhere in Peking.

As the New Year and the Moon Festival are the two most important holidays in the Chinese calendar, corresponding to Christmas and Thanksgiving, it is natural there should be a great many legends attached to them. The appearance of the rabbit is attributed to a myth in the Buddhist religion. In the days of the living Buddha there was a sacred grove where holy men went to meditate, and even the animals were affected by the sanctity of the spot. As the hare was the gentlest and most inoffensive among them, he was elected to read the sacred books and expound their wisdom to the rest. And since it was an appointment of honor rather than riches, the hare lived in poverty. One evening Buddha came to the grove with his disciples, to give them the fruit of his wisdom, and discoursed until the sun rose again in the sky; and when it was overhead, he changed his shape into a Brahmin, and cried out for alms, as though he had lost his way and was in distress. The animals of the forest, hearing his cries, brought him aid according to their resources; but the hare, having nothing, came forward empty-handed to the master, and declared he had only his body to offer as a sacrifice. So saying, he first combed his fur free of the denizens that lived there, that they should not be unknowing companions in his oblation, and then threw himself on a pyre of charcoal that had miraculously appeared beside him. The Buddha, moved by this sublime gesture of self-abnegation, declared that the hare should ever after be recorded in the lineaments of the moon, where, in Buddhist eyes, he is to this day.

The eighth moon is also the time of harvest, when our servants beat the chestnut trees so that the nuts, covered in their thick green husks, came raining down and the husks split open, revealing the light brown shells within. Roast chestnuts were sold on the streets, as well as ginkgo and pine nuts; and all kinds of delicious dishes were prepared at this season as a result of the wealth of harvest produce that poured into the city. Chicken, red-cooked with chestnuts and Chinese cabbage, was one of these, and appeared on our table; another consisted of a whole chicken stuffed with glutinous rice, chestnuts, ginkgo nuts, Chin-hua ham and black mushrooms. The rice was steamed first, with the chicken, and then the whole preparation was roasted, so that the bird was crisp outside. I believe the original way of cooking this was to deep-fry the chicken at the last stage; either way it was a superb dish. And pine nuts, sautéed with shrimp, were not to be despised.

For almost a month before the full moon, the confectioners' shops had been temptingly bedecked with the cakes always

170

eaten at the festival. Moon cakes were commonly given as presents in boxes of four. They were extremely rich and heavy in consistency, and full of ingredients symbolic of the fertility of the season—nuts, fruit, eggs and seeds—that were bound within a rich pastry of lard and gray flour. Each ingredient had its special significance: watermelon seeds stood for sons; lotus root for constancy; water chestnuts for posterity. Taro root, pear, chestnuts, persimmon, dates and a large amount of sugar might also be included, and in the south a duck egg and meat were sometimes inside as well. Our Peking moon cakes had less sweetening and were noticeably less rich than those in the south. The cake was baked to a golden brown outside and stamped with the emblem of the Moon Goddess.

Legend again surrounds the moon cake. It is said that in the last, decadent years of the Yuan dynasty, the women of Peking sent out messages concealed within the pastry they were preparing for the August Moon so that they could coordinate the forces for the uprising against the degenerate Mongol rulers, a stratagem which was eventually successful and opened the way to the Chinese rule of the Ming.

We always had a twelve-course banquet on the evening of the August Moon—of vegetables, of course, since it was the fifteenth of the month—and as there would be guests, we were especially well dressed and on our best behavior. Not that there was ever any question of being caught *en déshabille:* in those days everyone of any consequence was carefully dressed at all times, and although my married sisters or cousins would call without any previous notice, they would always have found us without a hair out of place. It was one of the merits of the family system that relatives could arrive for a meal and would be invited to stay as a matter of course. It was considered as merely a matter of an extra pair of chopsticks, although large formal lunch parties were unknown because of the custom of taking a siesta afterwards. Dinner was always the social meal to which specially honored guests were invited.

At the time of the August Moon, then, we expected to have a large family gathering, at which all my brothers and sisters, and their husbands and wives, would be present: in China children are always welcomed and always loved. Manners within the family were natural and simple. Although we did not have pocket money, we did not really need it; we had only to ask for something and it was provided. In the same way, we did not indulge in elaborate personal compliments when we met each other and only young schoolchildren made high-spirited personal remarks among themselves.

When guests arrived with gifts, it was considered most impolite to open them in front of the givers, for if one did not like the presents, it would be embarrassing to indulge in insincere thanks. On the other hand, it was absolutely mandatory to tip the servants after a dinner party or after playing *mah jong*, since tips were part of the natural and accepted perquisites of the domestic staff. Working like slaves, and very poorly paid, they understandably expected some extra recompense. (This custom has made it increasingly difficult to hire servants in Taiwan. When they are interviewed they ask such questions as "How many dinner parties do you give? Do you play much *mah jong?*" And without sufficient reassurance on these points, they are unwilling to go into service.)

Another admirable Chinese custom was that guests always left immediately after a dinner party, and there was no question of continuing the entertainment into the small hours. As the saying went, *K'o ch'ü chu-jen an,* "Guests leaving make host at peace."

We always had new clothes for special occasions, and for my brothers it always meant a haircut and a ceremonial bath. At the New Year, for instance, one had to wash oneself ritually all over before going to pray at the temple and make offerings.

At dusk we went out into the garden for *shang-yüeh*, "enjoying the moon." It was almost always clear and cold, the leaves had changed, and the air was still. The elders drank wine and ate nuts; and the jade rabbit and decorative flags, hand-painted with characters of good fortune, hung in the courtyards, barely stirring. My mother led us in *k'o-t'ou*-ing at the altar, which was set up outside with two red candles, an incense burner and a statue of Kuan-yin, and the maidservants and chambermaids knelt with us—but not my father, as this was a feminine ceremony, and men do not take part in worship of the moon.

We lighted a bundle of many sticks of incense, and put them into an incense burner, shaped like a flower pot, called *hsiang-t'ou*, and at the appropriate moment all the decorations and the Jade Rabbit were burned in one exciting holocaust, lighting up the faces of all the assembled throng. Our elders continued to sip warm rice wine and compose poems about the moon, which was now hanging like a golden ball in the sky. The moon always arouses the poetic instinct in the Chinese. The most famous celebrant of the August Moon (Chung Ch'iu) and the Moon Lady, was Li Po, who went to a watery grave as a result of trying to capture her reflection in a river after an evening of wine.

By the fifteenth day of the eighth moon, the immanence of darkness is felt to have outweighed the light, and the *yin*, or female principle, personified by the moon, is in the ascendant. This is why the August Moon is regarded as a female festival. Oddly enough, the Kitchen God, propitiated at the New Year, is tended only by men, and although women spend much of their lives in the kitchen, they do not take part in the ceremonies which speed him on his way to the Jade Emperor.

The vegetarian banquet was usually held after all the ceremonies of the moon viewing, but not in our family. We ate at our usual hour, which was a much more convenient arrangement for everybody and may well have been in deference to my father's wishes: he did not like to have his routine disturbed on account of religious observances.

Autumn, called *ch'iu-t'ien*, often has its Indian summer, or "autumn tiger" (*ch'iu lao-hu*), a spell of fine weather before winter sets in, and we looked forward to it as prolonging our outdoor activities. Every morning the sound of our singing birds could be heard through the house, or the talking parakeets, and we could play with the dogs and cats. We never took them for walks or fed them—that again was for the servants to do: we just had the pleasure of romping with them in the courtyards. My brothers had crickets, some of which they caught themselves, and trained them to fight by teasing them with little whisks poked through the bars of their little wicker cages. Sometimes my sisters and I bought silkworm eggs, which came on sheets of paper, and raised the worms on mulberry leaves, until we had them swarming everywhere, and finally weaving their silken cocoons about them. Some were yellow and some pure white. Further afield, we raised rabbits at Ch'ang-hsin Tien, where there were also all kinds of butterflies, which we sometimes mounted in frames. My brothers also used to catch lizards, but one had to be careful to avoid one variety, with a hooked tail, which was believed to be poisonous. And at the risk of upsetting some of my readers, I am reminded of a famous Tientsin specialty, grasshopper pie, in which the abdomens of the grasshoppers were *ch'ao*-cooked to make a crisp, crunchy and succulent filling for a *pao-ping*.

INTERLUDE
Dishes from a Mandarin Banquet

Descriptions of the large banquet *ch'iu-hsi*, or "wine spread," consisting of twelve courses, are in some ways misleading, as Western peoples often seem to imagine that the guests gorged themselves. In practice, one selected a morsel of a dish one liked, a mouthful or two at most, and sometimes skipped a course altogether. When the guests were assembled, they found dishes of nuts on the table—fresh, toasted almonds, pine cones *ch'ao*-cooked with a little sugar and pepper, cashew nuts and walnuts—which were eaten to the accompaniment of a slightly sweet plum wine, as an appetizer. After this leisurely introduction, during which the company grew more animated, the nuts were swept away, and the chef's art was first displayed in the form of a *leng-p'an*, or cold plate. This set piece might represent a phoenix or a landscape with figures and flowers, all contrived out of edibles, and evoked cries of admiration around the table.

Four *ch'ao*-cooked dishes, *chiu ts'ai* ("wine dishes"), now made their appearance: shrimp or lobster—rare in China except in the south—or crystal prawns. In the latter dish the prawn becomes quite transparent while retaining its characteristic taste. The second dish might be fresh winter bamboo shoots with, not merely snow peas, but the even more delicate sprouts of snow peas, *tou-miao*. Fresh, tender scallops would make the third dish, or velvet chicken, melting in the mouth; and the fourth dish could be sautéed chicken livers.

In Peking we usually followed the "wine dishes" with a major dish, such as shark fins whole, arranged like flower petals, with the yellow part of the female crab in the center. By now the wine served would have been a choice *Shao-hsing* (rice wine) suited to the delicacy of the food.

Points to notice are that out of politeness to one's guests, no dishes at banquets were seasoned to excess, too hot or too peppery, and no plain meat, that is, pork, was served, as being too common. All bones, skin and gristle were removed, so that one did not have to spit anything out. And rice, the staple food of so much of China, did not make an appearance at all.

The shark fin might well be followed by another delicacy, turtle soup. A basic chicken stock, made with the whole bird and some Chin-hua ham, provided a clear soup, in which the turtle meat, cut in large pieces, was slowly simmered over low heat. At the last stage a little good wine was added.

The eighth course introduced Peking duck, which I have already described at length, and will therefore pass to the next course, which was a special ham preparation. This was made from the center cut, which was coated with honey and a little wine, and then steamed. The combined flavor penetrated the meat, giving it a delicious flavor. It was then thinly sliced, and eaten as a sandwich, in a fold of a special kind of steamed bread.

Sea cucumber arrived next, sometimes sautéed with shrimp eggs and wine, or with abalone, ham and chicken—a delicate matching of flavors and textures, requiring great skill by the chef and an informed palate in the eaters.

For the tenth course, a steamed fish was placed on the table, cooked whole, so that gourmets could seek out their favorite portions, such as the "cheeks," the lips or the fins; and the flesh at perfection's point, neither dry nor clinging to the bones.

By this time the appetite of most of the guests was almost satisfied. To freshen the palate a soup was served, a light one, such as "three delicious," *san-hsien t'ang*, which is made in a number of variations on the theme of one seafood element and two others—abalone, chicken and ham; or prawn, chicken and ham; or dried scallop, chicken and ham—all shredded in a clear broth.

For the twelfth course, there might appear steamed *chiao-tzu* and small *pao-tzu*, variously filled, and as a finale, an almond float, and some fresh fruit. The rarest in China were grapes, which, with melon, would be the most luxurious combination. Guests would finally be dispatched with freshly brewed tea.

At least two of the dishes I have mentioned can be adapted for a Western-style lunch or dinner: the steamed fish and the three delicious soup.

STEAMED FISH
CH'ING CHENG YÜ

1 rock cod, carp, sea bass
or red snapper, 2–3
pounds
5 scallion tops, 4 inches
long
3 slices fresh ginger root,
¼ inch thick
garnish: 4 scallions, finely
shredded, and fresh
coriander

SAUCE
2½ tablespoons cottonseed
oil
3 drops seasame seed oil
3 or 4 drops light soy sauce
dash of Chinese cooking
wine

Make incisions one-half inch apart on both sides of the fish (as in preparing the fish on page 23). Arrange the scallions on a platter, and lay the fish on its side on top; stick the slices of ginger into the incision nearest the head.

Place the platter on a rack in a *wok* or roasting pan (having brought some water in the pan to the boil first). Cover, and steam for seventeen to eighteen minutes.

In the meantime, mix the cottonseed oil with the sesame seed oil, soy sauce and wine, and cook for two to three minutes to blend the flavors. When the fish is ready to be served, pour the sauce over it, and garnish with the scallions, shredded lengthwise, and some chopped coriander. The fish thus prepared has just sufficient seasoning to bring out, rather than mask, its delicacy, and in that respect is typical of the restraint of the northern Chinese cuisine.

THREE DELICIOUS SOUP
SAN-HSIEN T'ANG

2 medium-sized abalone	dash of Chinese rice wine or
1 bamboo shoot	dry sherry
1 dozen snow peas	pinch of sugar
2 boned chicken breasts	3 or 4 drops sesame seed oil
¼ pound Virginia ham	1 teaspoon cornstarch
2 tablespoons cottonseed oil	5 cups chicken stock
½ teaspoon salt	

As in most Chinese soups, the base is a good chicken stock, which I will assume you have available (see page 49). Now for the preparation. All the ingredients are to be matched in size and shape. First, trim off the curly edge of the abalone, slice thinly, and then into julienne strips. Slice the bamboo shoot into six or seven thin slices, then into julienne strips. Slice the snow peas lengthwise into julienne strips; then the chicken breasts and ham. With the ingredients all evenly matched, we proceed to plunge the chicken breasts into boiling water and remove immediately. A *wok* should be prepared by heating, and putting in it the cottonseed oil, coating the sides, and heating the oil to 375 degrees. Add the salt, and then throw in the bamboo shoot, the ham, the wine and lastly, the chicken. Quickly stir-fry for two minutes, and toss. Add the snow peas, the cornstarch (blended with a little water), the sugar and the sesame seed oil, and stir quickly to blend all together. The total cooking time should be approximately three minutes. Bring your chicken stock to the boil, turn off the heat, add all your ingredients to it in a beautiful bowl and bear it to your guests.

The name of this soup, *san-hsien t'ang,* is an amusing example of the allusiveness of the Chinese written language—and some may say, the elusiveness as well. The characters, from left to right, mean "three fish-lamb soup," of which the two characters for fish and lamb together signify "delicious." And as I observed earlier, seafood, in one form or another, is always an essential ingredient.

The two recipes above are comparatively simple to prepare and cook. If one has ambitions of trying one or two of the more difficult dishes appearing on a grand occasion, such as the sea cucumber with shrimp eggs or the preparation sometimes called chicken velvet, *fu-jung chi-p'ien,* the results are well worth the trouble.

SEA CUCUMBER WITH SHRIMP EGGS
HSIA-TZU HAI-SHEN

4 sea cucumbers
2 tablespoons cottonseed oil
2 tablespoons fresh shrimp
  eggs

1 tablespoon Chinese rice
  wine
3 fresh green scallions
2 tablespoons chicken stock

The sea cucumber, otherwise known as *bêche-de-mer* in French cuisine, or as trepang, is imported in dried form, and the best kind comes from Japan. It arrives only three inches long or less, and the thickness of a cigar and is dried quite hard. Soak the sea cucumbers in fresh, cold water for two days, changing the water every day, and making sure that there is no oil of any kind on your hands or in the vessel in which the sea cucumbers are lying, or they will not swell up. After two days they will have swollen considerably. Now put them into some lukewarm water, in which they will gradually soften, and one can then see the cucumber-like nodules on the upper side and the smooth belly underneath. Slice each one open and clean out the intestines thoroughly; then wash again in clean water. Put them into a pot, with enough water to cover, and simmer with the lid on the pot for twenty minutes. Remove from the heat and cool. Store in the refrigerator overnight, after changing the water again. The next day simmer in fresh water for another twenty minutes; the little bumps will have become still larger. The sea cucumbers are now ready for the final *ch'ao*-cooking. Cut each one in half lengthwise and then into one-inch pieces. Heat a *wok*, and coat the sides with the cottonseed oil and bring it to bubbling. Add the sea cucumber pieces, the shrimp eggs, the rice wine, scallions and soy sauce, stir-frying all the time, for about one minute. Now add the chicken stock and simmer for a couple of minutes more, and a classic dish has come into being.

There are several versions of the famous Chinese dish known as *fu-jung chi-p'ien*, sometimes translated as "chicken velvet," although literally meaning "egg chicken slices." Even that is not quite exact, as *fu-jung* is really a flower name used to indicate dishes cooked with egg. It often figured at banquets as a *hsiao-ch'ao*, or "small" *ch'ao*-cooked dish following the elaborate cold plate. The classic version for grand occasions

182

of that kind is really for the expert. It involves a complicated preparation, in which the chicken breasts are reduced to a paste by chopping and spreading the meat out with a cleaver until it is transparent, to reveal the white membranes, adding ice water, and marinating in egg white. There are more stages, to produce, finally, mouthfuls of snow-white chicken that drift lightly down the throat. I suggest that the following version is within range of the housewife and is delicious enough.

CHICKEN VELVET
FU-JUNG CHI-P'IEN

1 pair fresh, skinned
   chicken breasts
2 teaspoons ice water
2 cups cottonseed oil
½ cup chicken stock
pinch of salt
pinch of sugar
6 snow peas
6 button mushrooms

MARINADE
1 tablespoon cornstarch
   blended with water to a
   flowing paste
1 egg white
pinch of salt
dash of Chinese rice wine or
   light dry sherry

Pick out the tendon of each chicken breast with the point of a cleaver or knife, and lay the breast out flat on a board. Hold the cleaver almost parallel to the breast, spreading it out a little, and slice in half lengthwise. Scrape the meat into a paste, always along the breast in the direction of the fibers. Add the ice water at this point to make the paste even smoother. Put the chicken paste into a bowl with the marinade ingredients, and mix extremely thoroughly with the fingers to ensure a smooth texture, free from bubbles. Heat a *wok*, put in the cottonseed oil, and heat to 160 to 170 degrees. The

183

oil should not be hotter or the chicken will brown. The chicken paste should be placed in the warm oil in pieces about the size of a large almond, all at the same time, and cooked for thirty seconds. Scoop them all out. At this stage the pieces are cooked around the edges and already white, while the centers are still slightly underdone. Brush the oil out of the *wok* and put in the chicken stock, the salt and the sugar. Rapidly stir-fry the chicken pieces with the snow peas and button mushrooms. Alternatively, a little shredded Virginia ham can be added. This rapid *ch'ao*-cooking will take only another thirty seconds, when the dish should be borne to the table, admired for a few seconds, and then dispatched with celerity.

NINTH MOON

I SHOULD FEEL, I SUPPOSE, a certain proprietary interest in the ninth moon, as it was at this time of the year that I was born; and I always enjoyed Peking then for its dry, sunny weather, crisp, yet not too cold, when the chrysanthemum bloomed and the autumn leaves still blazed red and gold in Pei Hai. Many people used to go to the Western Hills, Hsi Shan, on the weekend, to make good use of this tranquil period before the onset of winter.

On the ninth day of the ninth moon, Ch'ung Yang, one was supposed to climb mountains, have picnics, fly kites, eat crab and drink some warm wine, which presented certain difficulties for northern city dwellers, as there were no mountains for miles around, and as yet very little wind for flying kites. One was not allowed to picnic on Coal Hill, the nearest approach to a high place available, nor to fly kites from it, but at least we could go to the highest place in the garden, the "man-made hill," and enjoy some warm wine impregnated with chrysanthemum petals.

The origin of the custom of mountain climbing is said to be the commemoration of Huan Ching, pupil of the soothsayer Fei Ch'ang-fang, who lived during the later Han period. Huan Ching had been warned to flee to a high mountain, taking his family with him, as well as food and chrysanthemum wine, with the added precaution of a bag filled with pieces of dogwood tied around his neck, in order to avert calamity for himself and all his kin. In Peking, for some reason, we flew kites only at the end of the New Year celebrations, although the Cantonese fly them assiduously at both festivals.

Just as the eighth moon is associated with the *yin*, or female principle, the Double Ninth, or *Ch'ung-yang Chieh*, is predominantly male, and being a pair, and therefore a lucky number, is thought auspicious for mountain climbing, *teng-kao* ("climb high").

We ate special *teng-kao* cakes at this time, a kind of pastry made of glutinous rice, filled with meat and flat in shape, which was made in a mold and then steamed. In the old days these customs had a particular significance for the official classes, as the chrysanthemum symbolized endurance and the word cake, by punning association, could also mean "promotion." Chrysanthemum-viewing parties were held by the Imperial Court in the grounds of the Forbidden City, and literati vied with one another in composing poems while sipping the life-lengthening wine.

My parents usually gave a family dinner party on the day of the Double Ninth, which took advantage of whatever fruits were in season and had no embargoes imposed by religion on meat or fish. Ceremony was always observed. The guest of honor, the most senior male relation, invariably sat on the far side of the room, facing the door, with my father opposite him; and when all the company was seated, my father would propose a toast to him, and everyone else was obliged to follow suit. On these occasions the finger game *ts'ai-ch'üan* would be played, in which one called out the sum of the fingers put out by oneself and one's opponent; and if one lost, the loser had to down his glass. Numbers themselves were thought too crude: each player would say, "One for Sure," "Three Stars," "Four Happiness," and so on up to ten, which is, of course, the limit of the two hands. For some reason, eight was known as "Eight Horses"—I never knew why. I was not allowed to play this game until after I was married, in Shanghai, although I became very skillful at it. You must play at the speed of lightning, or else you will continually pay the forfeit, and with practice you begin to know your opponent's way of thought.

Another drinking game consisted of reciting a verse of eight characters, which your drinking partner had to match exactly. This required no little literary skill. It could be played only by intelligent, well-read people, and was considered a polished social accomplishment.

While my father was expected to supervise the wine, which he poured personally from a silver vessel into silver wine cups—considered a precaution against poison—my mother was required by etiquette to offer especially delicate morsels to the guests and to see that they were well provided with food. As a result of the finger games, which were naturally noisy, even boisterous, the company was soon in a good mood —far from the picture of the calm, inscrutable Chinese often cherished in the West, and quite unlike the constrained manners of the Japanese.

Although we normally ate off bare tables of polished teak, or of marble edged with teak, on these special occasions the tables, large and round, seating eight each, were covered with embroidered cloths, either white with colors, or off-white with gray embroidery and with scalloped edges. In addition to a silver wine cup, each place had ivory chopsticks tipped with silver—again, an ancient protection against poison: silver was believed to turn black if it touched any envenomed food —a not altogether reliable test, for any egg dish would fail to pass it. At each place was a silver chopsticks rest, where they were placed between courses.

A soup bowl, a bowl for rice, a small dish for sauce or spices, and a small plate for bones, which one was expected to spit out—it was considered bad manners to touch the mouth with one's fingers—were all that was required to serve each person, with chopsticks and a soup spoon as the sole implements: excepting that a tiny, two-pronged fork sometimes appeared for spearing fruits or sweetmeats. No cocktails preceded dinner, and wine alone or hard liquor, without ice or water, accompanied the meal. If my father said, *"Kan pei"* ("Dry cup"), everyone had to drain his cup. This conviviality at table is highly characteristic of the Chinese, and distinguishes them once again from the Japanese, who, when they wish to drink, always leave their wives at home and go with men friends to a geisha house. The Chinese expect their families to share in any entertainment.

Each course, in banquet style, was served one at a time, with a fresh plate for each, and the dinner would pursue its course from appetizers to light dishes to "heavier," more elaborate preparations, ending with fish, soup and a dessert of fruit, always totaling an even number of courses—ten or twelve. Surfeit was avoided by eating with calculated discretion.

The wines served were not wines in the Western sense, as they were made, not from grapes, but from rice, millet, sorghum and other grains; yet they varied considerably in taste and strength, and the finest were aged many years in their earthenware jars. A favorite wine in Peking and the north in general was *kaoliang*, a strong, clear spirit made from the sorghum grown on the northern plains. Generally popular throughout China was the "yellow wine" (*huang-chiu*) usually called *Shao-hsing*, from the locality whence it came: it was obtainable in various grades, and it was always served warm, to bring out its flavor. *Mao-t'ai*, again called after a place name, was a strong millet concoction from Kweichow; Szechwan province furnished a powerful sorghum wine called *ta-ch'ü; fen-chiu* came from Shanshi, and *wu-chia p'i*, a wine tasting of herbs, again came from the north, and the best came from Tientsin. *Pai kan-erh,* or "white dry," was a very dry, extremely strong potion, often drunk with crab, to counterbalance the crab's "cold" nature. Many other varieties of wine were made by flavoring with fruit or flowers, such as *fo-shou chiu,* flavored and colored with pomegranate; *chu-yeh ch'ing,* colored like bamboo leaves; *mei kuei lu,* flavored with rose petals; or sweet wines such as *lien-hua pai,* with the informing fragrance of the lotus. We made many homemade wines in our household by adding fruit or flowers: plums, lemon peel, or rose petals occur to mind as obvious examples. A considerable range of medicinal wines were also concocted, fearsome distillations such as snake wine, into which the most venomous snakes were coiled, such as the cobra and the krait.

The crab season extends from September to November, and would certainly influence the menu of our Double Ninth dinner party. Nothing can compare with the Chinese fresh-water crab, greenish-black in color, for its infinitely delicate taste, of which the female comes in season first. My mother knew numberless ways of preparing them, such as steaming, served with a dipping sauce and garnished with ginger root dipped in brown sugar (a concomitant as necessary as a strong, warming wine because of the crab's "cold" nature). Crab might also be sautéed with ginger, or deep-fried in Wu-hsi style, with eggs and flour: the combinations were endless. When we were young the embargo on talking at mealtimes was always stringently observed whenever we ate seafood or shellfish because of the danger of choking on bones or shell— crab is often served in China with the meat attached to the shell on the principle "the nearer the bone, the sweeter the meat," a saw much quoted by my father.

In later years I also came to know the hairy sea crab of Taiwan, a small red variety, not known or seen in Peking. Whatever the kind, wine, sugar and ginger always went together with them, and so highly were crabs esteemed that it was not at all unusual to have parties especially devoted to them.

A particularly delicate flavor which makes its appearance at this time of the year is the sweet olive, or *kuei-hua*, with five-petaled, sweet-scented yellow flowers which blossom on black stems. The flowers were preserved in sugar, and were often added to foods—even to my father's tobacco—and made a rich-tasting sweetmeat in Canton when served with taro root in a thick syrup. This use of flowers in Chinese cooking is one of its most charming sides: in the ninth moon period the chrysanthemum pot makes its appearance as a seasonal dish, into which one dips seafood, and throws the petals of the flower into the basic soup. Rose petals, in their season, are employed as a filling for *ping*, or rose pie, with a touch of cinnamon, and in the spring, magnolia flowers are used to make a sweet pie called *yu-lan-hua ping*.

There was undoubtedly great style to the way of life in the thirties in the capital. The houses of the upper classes had quite unpretentious exteriors, and might well have an insignificant doorway and no windows opening on to the street; yet inside they could be of the greatest magnificence. The same rule applied to clothing. The people we associated with habitually wore quiet, dark clothes, often with a "long life" design, formed within a circle and woven in the same color as the material itself, which would, however, be of the finest quality and weave. Only very young children, or pregnant young wives, wore bright, patterned brocades: for everyone else a sober elegance was the invariable rule. I never saw my mother wear a print dress or bright colors, and I myself once owned as many as thirty black dresses at one time, in different weights and kinds of silk.

Polite forms of address were always used in speaking to elders and acquaintances. Our servants always called my father Lao Yeh, "Old Sire," for age conferred dignity; and ancestors often had their longevity improved upon on their ancestral tablets on the family altars, to increase their venerability and importance. My mother was similarly always addressed as T'ai-t'ai, or "Lady," the form of respect. We children, however, always called our father A-pa, and our mother Ma, corruptions dating from the time when our elder brothers and sisters could not pronounce the words properly. For general courtesies, one called people Hsien-sheng, "Before Born," as when one spoke of a geomancer as Feng-shui Hsien-sheng, "Wind and Water Before Born," or freely translated, "Mr. Diviner."

With this attention to formalities, it may seem strange that our family parties and banquets should have had the noisy prelude of finger games, verse matching and wine toasting, with the lively forfeit of draining one's glass; yet when everyone knew the rules—and on the whole the classes did not mix—there was an ease and freedom within the accepted framework of social intercourse which less conventional forms of society rarely experience.

INTERLUDE
Of Crab Banquets and Crustaceans

W̲HEN THE CRAB CAME INTO SEASON after the August Moon, we frequently dined on nothing else. A crab dinner had a name to itself, and no limit was set to the number of crab served; as with Peking duck, one ate as many as one felt inclined. We began, as I have noted earlier, with the female of the species, which was smaller than the male and had a delicate yellow part that was highly esteemed. Both were greenish-black in color, and the best came from near Shanghai. They were brought to the table steamed, and were served with dark rice vinegar, chopped ginger and brown sugar, and I have always found the claws and body especially good. My mother used to save the delicately flavored legs to sauté with eggs, or alternatively, to add to pork and use as a filling for *pao-tzu* or *chiao-tzu*. The yellow part of the female crab and the flesh were also combined with shark fin to make an opulent dish.

A distinct, variant preparation was drunken crab, for which very small, dollar-sized soft-shelled crab were used. First they were well washed, and their claws tied up with thin strips of straw. They were then immersed for days in a marinade of rice wine, a little star anise, rock salt and round black Szechwan peppercorns, until they were assumed to be thoroughly intoxicated, and then were eaten raw. One had to be careful that they were still alive, or they might have been dangerous to consume. These were called *tsui-hsieh*. This method was similar to the method of preparing *ch'iang-hsia*, or "dancing shrimp," which I have described, characteristic only of the lake near Wu-hsi. These shrimp had their legs and the pointed part of the head removed, and had poured over them a sauce of wine with a quantity of pepper, red-colored preserved bean curd, soy, a little salt, and plenty of ginger, which mixed all together made them jump, and earned them their culinary name. As they were strictly a local delicacy, we never ate them in Peking, and although my mother had spoken of them, I never tasted them until I visited my mother's home province after V-J Day. Another method of preparing crab, which I have named Crab Mandarin, is well adapted to the large kind found on the West Coast, and is a revelation to those familiar only with Occidental recipes.

CRAB MANDARIN
CH'ING CH'AO P'ANG-HSIEH

1 1-pound live crab
all-purpose flour
4 or 5 chunks fresh ginger
   root, 1 inch thick
6 green scallions cut in
   3-inch lengths
2 tablespoons cottonseed oil
½ teaspoon salt

½ teaspoon sugar
2 tablespoons Chinese rice
   wine or dry sherry
1 cup chicken stock (see page
   49)
2 teaspoons soy sauce
3 or 4 drops sesame seed oil
3 tablespoons cornstarch

Pull off the top shell and remove the sand pocket from the live crab. Rinse and clean the crab in cold water. Chop off and crack the legs, and divide the body into six pieces. Dip the crab pieces into a bowl of all-purpose flour, so that they are barely coated; shake off the excess.

Stir-fry the ginger and scallion pieces in the cottonseed oil for thirty seconds over high heat (375 degrees). In a separate *wok* drop the crab pieces into very hot oil, 400 degrees, and deep-fry for three to four minutes, then lift them out with a strainer, and add to the ginger and scallions in the first *wok*. Sprinkle the crab with the salt, sugar and rice wine; add the chicken stock, cover, and simmer for five minutes over moderate heat. Add the soy sauce, the sesame seed oil and the cornstarch (blended with water to make a smooth flowing paste). Cook and stir-fry a few moments more, until the liquid begins to thicken, and serve immediately.

Equally typical of the Chinese repertoire is steamed crab, which again uses ginger and wine, although in different proportions, and in contrast to the last recipe, which is complete in itself, makes use of a piquant dipping sauce, to be indulged in at the discretion of the eater.

STEAMED CRAB
CH'ING CHENG HSIEH

1 one-pound live crab
dash of Chinese rice wine
   or dry sherry
3 slices fresh ginger root,
   ⅛ inch thick

DIPPING SAUCE
2 slices fresh ginger root, ⅛
   inch thick

1 tablespoon chopped fresh
   Chinese parsley
   (coriander)
1 teaspoon sesame seed
   oil
4 tablespoons soy sauce
4 tablespoons "red"
   Chinese vinegar (see page
   21)

Pull off the top shell and remove the sand pocket from the live crab. Place the crab in cold water to cover for five minutes. Using a cleaver, chop off the legs at their junction with the shell, and chop the body into six pieces. Reassemble the crab

199

in its natural shape on a platter, having first cracked the legs; sprinkle with rice wine and place the three slices of fresh ginger on the body. Re-cover the body with the (well-rinsed) shell, and steam for fifteen minutes in a bamboo steamer, covered.

For the dipping sauce, crush the ginger, chop it finely, and put it in a bowl. Add the coriander, sesame seed oil, soy sauce and vinegar, and mix thoroughly. Guests should have a small saucer added to their place settings, so that they can help themselves to as much or as little of the dipping sauce as they choose.

Among the smaller shellfish, prawns produce elegant and delicate preparations, and I have always found the following recipe much appreciated.

SPIDER WEB PRAWNS
CHIH-CHU MING-HSIA

1 cup fresh prawns shelled and cleaned
1 teaspoon equal quantities mashed garlic and ginger
2 tablespoons cottonseed oil
2 tablespoons Chinese rice wine or dry sherry
2 ounces carrots, sliced in medium julienne strips

¼ pound bamboo shoots sliced in matching julienne strips
1 tablespoon hot bean sauce (see page 21)
dash of fagara oil (see page 161)
½ teaspoon cornstarch
½ teaspoon salt
½ teaspoon sugar

Heat a *wok* thoroughly, coating the sides with the cottonseed oil, and then remove most of it. Put in the garlic and ginger mixture to impregnate the oil, and then add the prawns and stir-fry vigorously. Add the rice wine, and while continuing to stir, the carrot and bamboo shoot slivers. *Ch'ao-* cook rapidly. Next, add the hot bean sauce, fagara oil, cornstarch (blended with a little water), salt and sugar. The prawns are cooked in about the time it takes you to follow the instructions; in other words, speed and dexterity should be your watchword. In China this dish was traditionally made with more vegetables in proportion to the prawns, which were an expensive delicacy.

TENTH MOON

THE FIRST TWO YEARS OF MY LIFE WERE SPENT, not in our spreading Ming Palace, but in a smaller house on two floors, near the Grand Hôtel de Pékin, adjoining the Legation Quarter. It had no tap water or well, and we depended for our supply on the delivery man, who trudged daily through the narrow streets, which during the colder months were almost invariably icy or snow-covered, pushing a wooden cart with a single pair of wheels. It was often burdened with four large barrels, which dripped and splashed at intervals, so that icicles hung from it in a glistening fringe. The carrier attached himself to the cart by means of a rope, which was padded with quilting and slung around his neck and over his shoulders; and the cart had legs, like an oversized wheelbarrow, enabling it to stand level when he was not dragging it along.

Our street was remarkable for an enormous tree, which effectively prevented anything larger than a rickshaw, carrying chair or motorcycle from getting by it, and it presented a formidable obstacle to our water carrier, who was obliged to edge perilously into a ditch in order to pass; yet no one dared to cut it down since it had the strange property of crying out and bleeding if anyone bumped into it or injured it. Because our larger home had a deep well and water pipes, we had no further need of the water carrier, although we often saw him pulling his cart through the streets, and pitied him for his heavy load.

Peking is cold in November. It is already the beginning of winter, or Li Tung; the trees are bare; there are no more autumn leaves; and in the morning the courtyards are white with hoar frost. We now wore our winter clothing, putting on extra layers as the weather became progressively more penetrating. We shivered at night in our starched sheets, with their uncomfortable seam down the middle, and if we had edged toward the corner of the pillow, we were apt to have traces of the stiff embroidery patterned on our cheeks when we first awoke. My father had taken the precaution of putting his prized *bonsai* into the little hothouse with its glass roof, which he had erected near the moon gate leading to the garden. Rows of little stoves, consuming much precious fuel, would carry his plants safely through the winter.

As a small child I was often secretly terrified during the winter months, while they ran their course in our vast, rambling old house. It was not a matter for worry during the daytime, as light and the bustle of people deflected one's fears, and the large stone spirit screen beyond the anteroom at the main gate was reassuring; but the days were shortening, and in the evening the huge rooms, with their high, coffered and painted ceilings, sparse, forbidding furniture and dim electric light, always seemed to hold a hidden menace. My younger sisters and I had to persuade servants to escort us when we wanted to go to another part of the house: we were too scared to make our way alone through the lamp-lit, creaking corridors. We were constantly being told to turn off the light as soon as we left a room, which only added to our fears, for who could say what might be lurking in the dark?

Many of the little-used rooms had altars bearing ancestral tablets. Our forebears were still worshipped in our house according to ancient custom, and each altar, draped in red and decorated with tassels and embroidery in gold, and bearing on the frontal the family name in gold thread, had rows of wooden tablets with the names of members of our race, to whom we brought offerings of their favorite foods and wines on the anniversary of their birth and death, and made a ceremonial *k'o-t'ou*. A large incense burner stood in the center of every altar, flanked by two large candlesticks with large red candles (white candles were used only at funerals). Cut flowers did not appear on the altars and are seldom seen anywhere in a Chinese house, growing plants being preferred, although flowers in cut paper are sometimes employed in decoration. The only famous ancestor I remember is one from whom my mother is descended: Hsüeh Fu-ch'eng, whom the elaborate system of ancestral tablets recorded for posterity. Usually the names of only the most immediate forebears were kept on the altars: the earlier tablets were eventually burned after being transcribed into a carefully preserved book.

When we went to pay our respects to our ancestors we knelt on the two red velvet cushions that rested on an angled frame in front of the altars, so that we could make the customary reverence in comfort: and we never questioned these ways, for we did not know any others. Brought up in obedience to tradition, we followed the pattern set for us.

On the first day of the tenth moon is the winter feast for all the spirits, when they are made comfortable for the dark days ahead with quantities of warm quilted garments, money, servants, and many other necessaries, all made out of paper. A carefully itemized list was included so that the spirits would know what had been sent them and could make sure that it had all arrived safely by checking the inventory. Everything was consigned to the flames to speed it on the way to the nether regions. This feast concluded the cycle dedicated to departed souls, which had begun with the joyful feast of Ch'ing Ming between the second and third moons, when family tombs were swept and garnished—the feast that coincides with the rebirth and resurrection of spring; had continued with the Feast of the Hungry Ghosts, in the seventh moon, when those poor wandering shades who had no pious descendants to mourn them were given offerings and shepherded back to their domain by the kindly Ti-t'sang Wang; and now was rounded off for the year by the Festival of All Souls.

As much of the house as was feasible was locked up during the winter, to conserve fuel for the most-used rooms and to keep in the warmth stored in the thick walls. For the same reason, when we were living without visitors, we dined in a room which my parents had built near the kitchens, across a courtyard at the back of the house, so that food could always arrive hot at the table. It had large glass windows in a more modern style than the other buildings, and looked out on one side at beautiful chestnut trees, and on the other, a group of blossoming *hai-t'ang*, as though one were eating out of doors; and it had space enough for two large round tables, seating eight at each. As soon as company came, though, the formal dining room nearer the front of the house came into use once more.

Old houses like ours often have secrets, and ours was no exception. In one part, on the garden side, a mezzanine had been built, reached by a stairway concealed behind a panel in the room below: the ceilings being so high, there was plenty of space for this intermediate floor. The chamber above it had exquisitely carved panels, each framing a painting, a beautiful survival of the original seventeenth-century decoration. An altar table was in position, with incense burners on it, to ensure the comfort of the inhabitant, for this had obviously been built for a *hu-hsien*, a fox. One did not talk about him or seek him out, or he might get up to mischief, although such foxes were usually friendly; and since he had been provided with a room of his own there was a good chance he would disturb no one.

The watchman, who paced all night around the house with the watchdogs in the narrow passageway allotted to his use, clapping out each hour of the night on his wooden bars, could sometimes be heard clearing his throat loudly, or ostentatiously spitting on the ground, as a polite notice to the fox, lest he tread on him by accident in the dark and incur his fairy wrath.

Foxes love children, and often play tricks on them: it was only recently that my son told me of experiences dating back to his early childhood, when we lived in a large and beautiful old house in Tokyo. The roof beams, of natural wood, were massive balks of timber which ran the entire length of the building, and the ancient floors had been rubbed constantly with walnut oil over the years so that they had a patina like satin; and we naturally followed the native custom of taking off our shoes on entering the house for fear of injuring the surface. In Japan, just as in China, old houses are often visited by foxes; and my son remembers the games they played on him: sometimes he floated through the air, and was carried into another room; sometimes he would go to sleep in one room and wake to find himself in another. And once, when he awoke feeling very cold, he saw his blanket floating in the air, and tried to drag it back to his bed on the *tatami* floor. He never said anything at the time for fear the servants would get him into trouble over it.

I never saw a fox while I was living in our Peking house, although I heard that one visited a woman who had rented part of the front of our house during the war. She was told by the fox to put out good food and wine for him near the stalls for the carriages at the front gates.

A number of houses in Peking were haunted by ghosts and stood empty, well known and shunned by rickshaw boys, real estate agents and taxicab drivers, as well as everyone in the surrounding neighborhood. An American rented one of these once, pooh-poohing the stories that circulated about the building, and installed himself. It was not long before he changed his tune. The visitants continually plagued him, moving him from room to room until he finally owned defeat after being locked into one of them, and being unable to escape until someone came to rescue him.

My mother, as a strict Buddhist, refused to acknowledge the existence of foxes, and equipped our mezzanine room with shelves, on which she stored all the impedimenta of a large household: trunks filled with light and heavy furs; spring, summer, autumn and winter clothes; shoes; hats; scroll paintings (our walls had their pictures constantly changed, unlike the Western ways of decoration); but it was not a room to which I would willingly have ascended, up its little secret stair.

Spirits are ever present in Chinese life. It is generally believed that when someone dies, his soul comes back on the third day, embodied in the phrase, *chao-hun*, which means literally, "soul come back." And I was present once when this belief was put to practical use. The Chinese rarely make wills until the very last moment, and therefore they leave it sometimes too late, and there is confusion about the wishes of the deceased. When this happens, the family leave the door open and scatter a pathway into the house of fine white sand, leading to a room where the favorite foods and wines of the departed are laid out. Then at dusk the soul returns and enters the body of one of the waiting relatives, who speaks with his voice and answers questions regarding the disposition of the estate. Then when all are satisfied, the soul floats away again, leaving only faint, yet discernible traces on the fine white sand. And this I saw, with my own eyes.

We believe also that those who are killed prematurely, as

in an automobile accident, are heard moaning near the scene of the tragedy; these unfortunates are known as *yüan-kuei,* or "complaining ghosts," as they regret their lives were cut short. And there are also the *wu-ch'ang kuei,* or "unpredictable ghosts," as they sometimes materialize and just as inexplicably disappear. At school we frightened each other with stories of ghosts which some claimed to have seen: terrifying apparitions with faces like *tou-fu*—white, shapeless bean curd—and with no arms or legs; and as the bathroom at school was in an outbuilding at the far side of the school yard, there were many alarming tales which made one fearful of going there at dusk. Szechwan, in western China, is especially rich in ghosts, and when I lived there, tales of rickshaws moving in the streets but drawn by no one, sent a shiver down the spine.

Many places in Peking are reputedly haunted, like T'ien Ch'iao, which I went to only once before leaving the city, in order to find a battered old suitcase. I have described this sinister quarter elsewhere, a place where stolen goods were sold at dawn, and jugglers entertained the loitering passers-by, and pickpockets plied their trade. It had another, and more evil reputation, as a place of execution. Criminals were lined up against a wall with their names pinned up above, and had their heads chopped off. And no one ventured near there after dark: the ghosts of the executed lingered there, trying to attract the attention of the living, to plead they had been unjustly sentenced and were innocent of the crimes of which they were accused.

Since the dead are often laid in temples, those precincts, too, are much frequented by ghosts, who are said to gossip there, and play *mah jong,* in the still watches of the night. In common parlance, ghosts frequently make their presence felt. When a traveler loses his way, we say, *"Kuei ta ch'iang"*—a ghost has put a wall in front of him. And witches, *yeh-ch'a,* are also recognized: "witch" is a common term of abuse for a scolding wife or an unusually ugly woman. Battlefields are always teeming with ghosts, the spirits of warriors whose end has come too soon.

In the thick walls of our house there was room for many mysteries. My mother had several closets made, concealed in the breadth of the walls by the door jambs; just as in the Imperial Palace in the Forbidden City, whole chambers had been hollowed out, from seemingly solid areas, by successive Emperors of the Ming and Ch'ing dynasties. No sound from the street ever penetrated into our house. The windows all faced inwards, on to the interior; and I am often reminded, in thinking back about those days, of an old Chinese saying: *Shen-kung nei-yüan*, "The palace is so deep, you cannot even see the courtyard."

Five and a half years of my life were spent in Peking in the increasingly darker days of the Japanese occupation. The bombing of our properties in the south and the confiscation of our lands, stores and cinemas took their toll of the family fortunes; and we retreated further and further back into our house until all we occupied was the last and deepest court-yard. It was symbolic: for even exposure to the realities of war and the privations of living under an oppressive dominance did not really change our basic ways or habits of thought, and we believed optimistically in better days to come when all would be as it was before. There were those who betrayed their country, of course, and accepted the Japanese yoke, like the puppet Emperor of Manchukuo and some of his relations; but after all, the dynasty of the Ch'ing had not been Chinese, but invading Manchu, and the majority of my countrymen watched and waited with immemorial patience, cheered by any news they received of successes by the Nationalist troops.

INTERLUDE
Of a Family Dinner and
Firepot Cooking

I f one saw the words Hui Chao or Ch'ing-chen Chiao outside a restaurant in Peking, one knew it was a Mohammedan establishment, and therefore no pork would be served within its walls. Restaurants serving Peking duck and the Mongolian firepot were almost invariably run by Mohammedans.

At the firepot restaurants, the first sound one heard was the musical rhythm of cleavers chopping: the cooks were kept continually busy preparing to each diner's order the particular cut of meat—beef or lamb—he liked best. The huge joints were divided up and the meat sliced so thinly that it curled naturally into a roll, and one was charged by the plateful.

The firepot is a splendid dish to offset the winter's cold, and since most of the ingredients are cooked by each person individually at the table, yet in the same pot with the other diners', the pot itself becomes a warm and friendly centerpiece for a winter's dinner for the family. The nature of the firepot really requires a round table, seating six to ten people, with a *chuan-p'an*, or turntable, in the middle. The pot consists of a large metal bowl with a receptacle for a charcoal fire underneath and a funnel that rises in the center of the bowl and circulates the heat.

A firepot party is ideal to have, either for the family or for guests, if the number to be served does not exceed ten. With everyone cooking in the pot at once, as though fishing in a round pond, "pot space" is necessarily limited. All the ingredients to be cooked are laid out decoratively on plates around the firepot, and one dips one's choice into the hot soup until it is judged cooked. The method is known as "plunging" or "rinsing" (*chün*) since the hot soup in which the food seethes, cooks it in a few seconds, the time varying a little according to the ingredient. Traditionally, one is supposed to pick up the food in chopsticks and hold it in the soup; but if this is too difficult, wire strainers with long handles can be used.

In China an absolutely essential concomitant of the firepot was a large quantity of garlic, pickled in vinegar and sugar. The aroma, or effluvium, depending upon the point of view, of raw and pickled garlic penetrated every nook and cranny of the dining rooms, and was wafted upon the breeze by every guest on leaving the establishment.

Today, in the West, we can be a little more circumspect, and also enlarge the menu to include chicken and Virginia ham; and in addition to a plate of lamb, I have added a number of other ingredients which would not have been included in the northern Chinese version of this dish.

FIREPOT
HUO KUO

THE SOUP
1 3-pound chicken
1 fresh ginger root
6 large thick black dried
   mushrooms

4 ounces Virginia ham
1 pound Chinese cabbage
6 cups cold water
2 tablespoons Chinese rice
   wine or dry sherry

Chop the chicken cleanly into chunks two inches square, making sure not to splinter the bones. Peel and slice the ginger

216

into thin slices one-eighth of an inch thick. Reconstitute the mushrooms by soaking (see page 48) and drain. Remove the outer leaves of the cabbage; wash and separate the inner leaves. Combine all these ingredients in a large pot, bring to a boil, and simmer for one hour uncovered. When the scum has been removed, the soup is ready to go into the firepot, which is heated with charcoal or alcohol from beneath.

The firepot has a central funnel, or chimney, and if you need to reduce the heat at any time—when the liquid shows signs of boiling—you can put a saucer of water on top of the funnel, thus cutting off the draft.

While the soup is simmering, there is time to prepare the food which is going to be cooked in it:

1 pound lamb	2 dozen large shrimp
2 dozen large oysters	¼ pound spinach leaves

The lamb should be cut as thinly as possible, in strips about one inch by one and a half inches. If the oysters are particularly large, they should be cut in half. The spinach leaves must be thoroughly washed to remove any grit. All these raw ingredients should now be arranged attractively on dishes around the firepot.

The guests may now seat themselves at a round table, with the firepot simmering gently in the middle of it, and each selects a slice of lamb, or an oyster, or whatever he likes, and dips it into the broth until the meat changes color: it does not take long to learn the moment of perfection for each ingredient. And there is a further pleasant prospect before eating— a dipping sauce for which a small saucer at each place setting is needed.

TEN INGREDIENT SAUCE	Chinese vinegar
Chinese rice wine	sesame seed oil

sesame seed paste	bean curd cheese (*fu-yü*)
Chinese fresh chives,	fresh coriander
chopped	hot pepper oil (see page 161)
pickled garlic, chopped	shrimp sauce

All these condiments are set out in bottles or on plates. The quantities are immaterial, as each diner mixes the sauce in what proportions he pleases. If one does not like a fiery sauce, the hot pepper oil should obviously be used sparingly.

After the first pangs of hunger have been assuaged, and most of the raw foods on the plates have been dangled in the pot and devoured with suitable expressions of enjoyment, there comes the appropriate moment to add some new ingredients. There is now a residue in the bowl of marvelously enriched soup, flavored by all the edibles that have been cooked in it during the meal. Add to it five ounces or so of transparent noodles (which have been soaked in hot water for twenty minutes to soften), and while your guests are enjoying this unexpected development, put a fresh egg for each guest to poach in the soup, as a final course.

This dish is really sufficient for a complete dinner, but if some younger guests clamor for a dessert, some preserved fruits or a dish of almond bean curd, that is, something quite light, would be appropriate.

Other parts of China have produced hot pots of various kinds, such as the chrysanthemum pot of southeastern China, or the sandy pot of Chekiang, made of earthenware, or the porcelain pot of Yunnan with its steam vent. The last two are covered utensils, although the cooking methods are different. The sandy pot approaches the Occidental stew, and one may find in it bean curd, black mushrooms, abalone, bean sprouts, water chestnuts, and meatballs or a codfish head, with a chicken stock base: it is an excellent family dish, with its varied nutriments and wholesome soup—a regional preparation which one does not find in restaurants in the West.

The Yunnan pot is a little more sophisticated, as the food is steamed by means of a funnel rising in the middle of the vessel. The chrysanthemum pot is a wider, flatter kind than the northern firepot, and is usually heated with denatured alcohol, or methylated spirit as it is called in Europe. It differs relatively little from its Peking counterpart, except that more fish is introduced into the broth, and it receives a final topping of white chrysanthemum petals. It is often prepared in systematic layers, starting with Chinese cabbage, next fried bean curd, then chicken and meat, and finally fish balls; lamb is conspicuous by its absence.

One other Peking method of cooking that makes good use of lamb is the firepit, which can be used indoors and out. Lamb is cooked over charcoal on an open grill, under a layer of scallions, and then sandwiched in a sesame-seed *ping*. Inside a house you need a proper flue to take off the heat and the smoke; outside, it is the Chinese equivalent of the barbecue. Either way it produces a wonderfully savory-tasting meat, and I often used to see people, crowded around an improvised firepit made from an old oil drum lined with clay and set up in a Peking street, sitting on benches and munching contentedly, warmed by the fire meanwhile.

ELEVENTH MOON

LIFE IN PEKING became more alarming day by day. Apart from the inconvenience of losing our servants—we were now reduced to a cook, a maid and a rickshaw boy—and the commandeering of their quarters by the Japanese, we were subjected to all kinds of harassment by the authorities, and rationing had become increasingly severe. All the best food was kept for the Imperial soldiers. For the Chinese people there was no rice, no wheat flour: only rice husks and the husks of green peas. One had to take what was offered for the meager allowance of coupons, and there was little choice. No longer did the trains pour the delicacies of every province into the capital: transport was now reserved for the army, and Peking had to rely on the lands immediately around it for supplies. Those who had gardens began raising vegetables, and my father gave up some of the space devoted to his *bonsai* and flowers to provide fresh vegetables for the household. Money had become almost worthless: one had to pay tuition in gold or rice, and our properties, like the stores and movie houses, our country place at Ch'ang-hsin Tien and possessions at Wu-hsi, were either confiscated or damaged by bombing. For the first time in my life I encountered the problems of shopping for food—something I had never been required to do before—and would bring back something on my bicycle to augment our miserable rations. This was, of course, a black

223

market venture: I went to our former suppliers and bargained for wheat flour, rice, pork and sugar, not by the pound or the sackful as in the past, but something short of a pound—as much as could be safely hidden under one's clothes; for if one were caught, one risked being shot out of hand. It was still possible to eat in restaurants, but they were very expensive, and being rationed also, they provided food only as long as it lasted each day, and then closed.

At high school we noticed that some of our friends were disappearing, and we did not dare to ask where they had gone. Boys discussed leaving more openly, but the girls were secretive and perhaps more apprehensive; in any event we all felt we were increasingly a burden to our families. Finally, my Number Five sister, Sun Chin and I, decided, in the winter of 1942–1943, to make our way alone to Free China. Even as the crow flies the border was about five hundred miles, but we planned to go still further, to seek out our uncle, General Ting Gin, in Chungking, some two thousand miles by road and rail. The shortage of food was becoming acute, and we were fired by a naïve, but genuinely felt patriotism: we hated the Japanese, and wanted to live in a free China. I do not believe we had any conception of the dangers, still less the reality of the difficulties we might have to face. At that time one did not plan ahead or one might lose courage; one had to face each moment as it came. Absolute secrecy was necessary, and the consent of our parents. We were not at all sure how they would receive our plan, but their reactions were typical. My mother was horrified and wept copiously at the thought of her daughters leaving home—it was against all custom— and she could not conceive of our considering such a step. My father, in his usual broad-minded way, said it would be a new and valuable experience for us both; we were sensible and intelligent, and he felt sure we would be all right. My father's words settled the matter, and without mentioning anything

224

to relatives or friends, we began preparations. It is astonishing to me now to think how ignorant we still were of the world outside. We had seven pieces of luggage, made of *papier-mâché* bound with leather, containing the appropriate clothes for all four seasons, including our best dresses and fur coats, and fourteen pairs of shoes. In all fairness to myself I must admit that all seven suitcases were not exclusively for my sister and me. My mother had bethought herself that my Number One and Two sisters, now married and already in Yunnan, in Free China, might have difficulty in getting good clothes and be short of money to buy them; clothes for them too were packed with the rest. In taking so much we were also assuming that we should therefore not have to buy clothes on the way. We took soaps—very few cosmetics—thick cotton hose, and silk hose for evening wear (I never had any nylons until I bought a pair a year later in Chungking at what were called "hammer" (that is, auction) shops—*p'ai-mai hang*—at the inflated price of forty dollars a pair). Because we knew that at some points we should have to walk over very rough roads, my mother had had made for us very thick-layered, cotton-soled shoes, stitched and over-stitched, with white cotton tops, which were exceptionally comfortable.

We finally left Peking at the beginning of January, 1943, before dawn. My parents and my Number Eight sister (the only one left at home, as my Number Three was at T'ang-shan, in the outer suburbs), and the cook, maid and rickshaw boy, all said farewell to us in the darkness. We were torn with conflicting emotions: excited by the prospect before us; troubled by the thought we might never see our parents or our home again. We left at the earliest possible hour, as the Japanese made everyone register, and soldiers came each month to ask how many servants we had; even dogs and cats and food had to be declared. And knowing the fondness of Chinese for visiting, the authorities would always ask whether there were any house guests; and before one went anywhere, one was supposed to report to the police. In our case, my parents had simply decided to say we were out.

It was a hurried leave-taking at the main gate, my mother weeping, my father as gentle and unemotional as ever; and we climbed into a hired rickshaw, with the rickshaw boy's quilted coat across our knees instead of the fur rug we were used to. The rickshaw made no noise over the fallen snow, and the hood was up and the blind drawn down over the front, so that we were invisible from the outside: through a vent we could peek out and try to make out landmarks, for the last time. It was bitterly cold, so that we were glad of the protection of our fur-lined clothes and the almost hermetically sealed vehicle speeding us to the station. The train was crowded with Japanese soldiers, with little room to sit down, and the luggage was placed by a porter in another part of the train. We had disguised ourselves as peasants, covering our heads in blue and white scarves, and wearing grayish-blue jackets. We felt very tense—a strange mixture of exultation and fear and grief—excited by our mission, alarmed by the proximity of the Japanese soldiers, with their murderous-looking short knives, and thinking longingly of our home and family. Over and over again we rehearsed in our minds the answers to any questions we might be posed: where were we going, where had we come from, what was our business? And because any movement by the Chinese was regarded with suspicion by the Japanese, we always said we were going a short distance: this was to be our practice throughout, to suggest we were going only to the next village.

The route of the P'in Han railway took us first south and a little eastward, to Tientsin, then onwards across the north China plain and the province of Hopeh, to Tehchow, at the border of the province of Shantung, and on south, across the vast plain of the Hwang Ho, the Yellow River, to Tsinan.

226

Of food on the train there was none; all we could procure was *wonton*, and tea from an itinerant vendor, whenever the train stopped at a station.

Money was a special problem. The Japanese had printed paper money which changed in each province, so that they could keep a check on movements by the local population. Foreseeing this difficulty, we had provided ourselves with very small gold bars, which were sewn into our underclothes. Because there were frequent checkpoints, we had to be alert for any questions and hope we would not be too rigorously searched. Our peasant garb was an effective cover for our fur-lined clothes, which we dared not take off.

Our uncomfortable train continued on its way for almost a week and a half, until it finally crossed the Yellow River itself, the river commonly called the "Sorrow of China" because of the devastating floods which take toll of lives and crops year after year, sweeping away the precious "loess" and leaving farmers to starve. This terrible, now fast, now slow-moving river, with its dangerously high banks, looks like so much yellow mud at this point of its course, so that one could not believe any fish could survive in it.

From the junction of Tsinan, which is on the far side of the Yellow River, the line continues southwards across Shantung to where Hsüchow lies in the northernmost tongue of land in Kiangsu. Hsüchow marks the division between the north and south of China, and its border people have the roughness, even to their harsh pronunciation, which seems to typify all borderlines and boundaries. Among these rough folk we felt even farther away from the Peking we had left; and now we had to change trains, wearily lugging our suitcases, to go westward, toward our goal of Free China, to Shangkiu in Honan, near where some of the worst flooding of the Yellow River occurs. We were getting close to the firing line, and now disaster struck. The Japanese soldiers at Shangkiu robbed us of our luggage, and we were desperate. As so often happens in the chaos of war, we ran into a friend, Kao Lau-shi, one of the teachers from our high school, who offered to help us. I had already, before meeting him, summoned up courage to go to the local military command, where I had been interviewed by an evil-looking Korean with a twisted scowl, who had hinted darkly, and not too subtly, that for a bribe he would get our luggage released. We did not dare to take him up on this, as we did not have enough money, and certainly did not wish to arouse suspicion by offering him gold. Mr. Kao thought that his professional status might help in negotiating; but after waiting on tenterhooks for nearly a week, we were advised by him that it would be dangerous to stay on as the army was on the move, and our continued presence would arouse suspicion. I knew which unit had stolen our luggage because I had been able to read the characters on the soldiers' uniforms, identifying them, but it was useless and foolhardy to try any more.

We were now reduced to a very small supply of money and our carefully hoarded gold, but otherwise had nothing more than what we stood up in, and a washcloth and a toothbrush, and the worst part of our journey still lay ahead. Between Shangkiu and Kaifeng lay the neutral zone, defended on each side by deep anti-tank ditches, which at this time of the year, as the thaw set in, were wet and slippery. The area was doubly dangerous, as it was infested with bandits, acknowledging no law, civil or military; and on either side, ready to fire at the least sign of any movement, were long lines of Japanese and Chinese machine-gun posts. Fortunately, we managed to hire a guide who spoke both Chinese and Japanese, and knew the country and the relatively safe routes. We were thankful to find him, since we had heard many stories of girls being attacked, and were afraid of what might happen to us. Afraid is perhaps not the right word; one cannot live in constant fear and take action: one could not stop to think; each move, each step, needed a decision on the spot, and we could not think beyond the immediate moment. Everywhere, permeating everything, lay the half-frozen yellow mud, in which we slipped and stumbled. We had to be hauled across the anti-tank ditches with ropes, like so many balks of timber, and we grew filthier and filthier from our constant sliding in the yellow mud, which clung to us and caked our clothes. And we had other problems to face: in this part of Honan are several tributaries, as well as the old watercourse, of the Huang Ho, and we had to hire a sampan, with gold, to cross them all. Once on the far bank we still had the icy (and uneven) tracks to contend with. Sometimes we were able to ride on a farm cart, drawn by an ox or the farmer himself—in this region the carts have low sides, like beds on wheels—and we ourselves sometimes rode on top of the farmer's produce, remorselessly shaken and bumped and joggled by the springless motion over the frozen ruts. Three hours of sunshine succeeded in softening the icy way, after which it froze again into lumps and hollows, to increase our discomfort. Every day was punctuated with the sound of gunfire, and the dull crump of bombs exploding in the distance, or machine-gun fire from low-flying planes, slowing up our progress and forcing us to take cover.

As the weather grew a little warmer, and February stretched into March, we had to tie straw around our shoes, or else the yellow mud, which penetrated everywhere, would have pulled them off. We had not dared to carry a map with us, lest the Japanese find it and shoot us as spies, so we had to ask at each cluster of huts the way to the next village, and we were often lost. It was not unusual to find that the local peasantry did not know the name of the next town; they had lived their hard lives on the land they knew and tilled, and had never moved from it. We stopped at sunset and slept in whatever meager accommodation there was—in the hay in a farmer's barn if the village did not boast an inn—as it was not safe to travel after dark. We would get up at five or six o'clock in the morning, at the first light, eat a little *man-t'ou*, the big, steamed loaves of bread, typical of this region, drink some tea, and then walk on, making sure to reach the next village before nightfall.

Finally, after experiences I can only recall but cannot recapture—one's mind fortunately blots out some memories—we reached a little border town called Jiezhou, and crossed into Free China and wept aloud. It was a moment of intense emotion. We cried, "This is our country!," and gave full vent to our feelings after all the pent-up months of dissimulation, of walking, stumbling, running, hiding, in which we had been buoyed up only by our single-minded desire to be with our own free people again. We had arrived still in our fur-lined clothes—they were unbearably hot now that it was early May —and were covered with filth: we had never been able to wash or bathe or change; and we were as covered with lice as any beggar in Peking. The Chinese soldiers came to welcome us, plying us with questions, bringing us food and tea. Presently a soldier came up, followed by an officer, who asked us where we were from, and offered to help us as soon as we had explained ourselves. We were completely exhausted by this time with fatigue and excitement, and followed the officer to a student hostel, little more than a tent with a canvas bed, where we were able to wash for the first time and rest a little. We soaked thankfully in a Chinese tub, low and wooden, with a metal rim, rather like a planter. The tub was filled with bucket upon bucket of boiling water, and then cooled to a bearable temperature with cold. My face seemed to peel off, after all the exposure to wind and sun; and at last we were able to remove the fur-lined clothes we had worn under our quilted cotton throughout the journey.

In the evening, refreshed and rested, just as we were going to the dining room, we were met by another soldier, bearing a letter. To our amazement, it was from one of the girls at my high school, considerably older than either of us. She had left before graduating and had married General Chow, now in command of all the border forces. Personal names are so little used except between relatives that I do not think I ever knew hers, but nevertheless she had been informed of all our movements, through the mysterious grapevine of army intelligence, and knew everything we had gone through. She insisted that we stay with them. Travel-stained as we were, with no clean clothes to change into, we felt humiliated by the figure we cut, and thinking we should lose face if we accepted, gave a polite refusal. The soldier, however, said there was a military telephone we could use if we changed our minds, and departed. He soon returned, with a still more pressing invitation, and an even more welcome change of clothes, as well as soap. Madame Chow had provided us with attractive Chinese clothes of flowered cotton, for it was now very warm, like summer, and the aide waited while we changed, and escorted us to our new host, as curfew was at about eight o'clock.

General Chow and his wife were wonderfully kind to us. The General, six feet two inches tall, was an impressive figure, and his wife also was unusually tall, their height accounted for, perhaps, by the fact that they were both Manchus. The General overwhelmed us with compliments, saying he was amazed by what he described as our bravery—he had never heard of anything to compare with our journey—and offered to do whatever we asked. Furthermore, he wanted to adopt us; but we pointed out gently that as far as we knew, our parents were still alive: so he compromised by becoming our godfather.

We stayed with General and Madame Chow for some two weeks. Their house was a simple, temporary affair of brick and plaster, with brick or tamped-down earth floors and rattan beds. The food, typical of Honan, was comparatively simple, but seemed like luxury once more after our travels. The large, steamed loaf, or *mo*, a variety of vegetables and the "sandy pot," a splendid stew in which meat and vegetables mingle with noodles, were the principal dishes I remember, and the Chows had a most wonderful chef, Ch'u shih-fu, who introduced me to some ways of preparing noodles I had never seen before. He would hold the noodle paste in one hand and chop it as it reached the cutting board into paper-thin strips known as "knife-cut noodles"—*tao-hsiao mien*—which were put into soup. He would also make little, fish-shaped noodles —my mother knew them—by skimming paste with chop-sticks off the top of a tilted bowl; or "cat's ear," *mao erh-to*, of very thin dough broken off by hand and pressed with the thumb so that the edges curled up like ears. Sometimes we had the famous carp, *li-yü*, from the Huang Ho, although we were too far inland for any other fish or seafood.

After our recent experiences our life now seemed almost normal, but the war was never far away. One evening there was such a beautiful moon that the General suggested he should take us to a pleasant spot for moon viewing, and we climbed delightedly into his automobile. Before we were half-way to the elected spot, some Japanese planes came over, and we heard the ominous rattle of machine-gun fire: the planes always swept low. We flung ourselves out of the car and hid in some tall corn; and as we lay concealed, my sister began to call for me: "Number Seven, where are—where are you, Number Seven?" I was so terrified I could not answer, my teeth were chattering. When my sister eventually found me she said it was the noise of my chattering teeth that had given away my hiding place. In the towns, of course, warning systems were in force: one red lantern meant that planes were approaching; two red lanterns, that they had arrived; and three, that bombing had started and one should take cover.

And yet it is the yellow river mud that colors my whole memory of that time. I used to see women washing garments, pounding them on the rocks—to have them emerge dyed yellow; and I was astonished to see so many kettles thrown away in villages, until I realized that the deposit had caused the bottoms to break away, from the sheer weight of the encrusted clay.

Our journeying continued, first to Kaifeng, which is uniquely interesting because it still houses a Jewish community, settled there reputedly since the Sung dynasty, and thence along the border of the Yellow River to Chengchow. If there was a bombing raid on the way, we had to take cover in a field or, as we moved on into hilly and even mountainous country, find temporary shelter in a cave. One could hear, and sometimes see, heavy army trucks in the distance and the Japanese planes sweeping low whenever they spotted movement on the ground. We passed through Lo-yang, where there are many monuments of ancient Emperors, and T'ung-kuan, at the foot of the Hua-shan range, along the San-men Gorge. Food was very scarce in the mountainous regions, for Shensi, which we had now reached, is a poor province, with the extremes of climate that come from being so far inland, so that it is extremely cold in winter—it borders on Chinghai and Mongolia—and warm in summer. Here we encountered Moslems who offered us lamb stew and the large flat buns known as *mo-mo*. The stew is prepared with very little lamb and a great deal of spice and ground black pepper, so that it almost numbs the tongue.

Food became scarcer the higher we went, and I was astonished to see that many people had huge growths beneath their chins, the goitrous swellings which result from the lack of natural iodine in the diet or the water of the icy, glacial streams. I remember inquiring at one village whether there were any eggs, only to be told, "This week our hens produced only two eggs; you can have one egg, for one silver dollar." For the most part, the only food to eat in this region was a paste of water and wheat flour, cooked in an iron pot over a log fire, without salt or sugar: the most unappetizing food one can imagine, until hunger conquers one's distaste.

Although we were now traveling under the safe conduct of General Chow, the Japanese were still at our heels, and as we moved on, they were occupying towns we had recently left. At this time, General Chow had his home in Sian, the capital of Shensi (Shensi means "west of the pass," that is, west of the T'ung-kuan Gorge. Shansi means "western hills," and Shantung, "eastern hills"; between the latter two provinces lies the floodplain of the Huang Ho). Sian was therefore our next goal, as we continually moved upward into more and more rocky and mountainous terrain. It was at Sian that Chang Hsueh-liang, the Young Marshal, son of the Governor of Manchuria, Chang Tso-lin, had once held Chiang Kai-shek prisoner; and earlier, at the beginning of this century, it was to the rocky fastness of Sian that the Empress Dowager Tz'u-hsi had fled while the allied forces occupied Peking. We reached Sian in the middle of May, and stayed for a little over two weeks, but Generalissimo Chiang Kai-shek was in Chungking, our uncle, General Ting Gin, was in Chungking, our money was running short, and bidding farewell to General and Madame Chow we set out once more. The war was still too close to us in Sian, however protected by its precipitous natural defenses. General Chow's wife and his son stayed on in Sian, and I heard from them no more.

Not far from Sian was Yenan, where Mao Tze-tung had his cave headquarters, together with Chou En-lai, and Generals Lin Piao, Chu Tieh and Peng Teh-hwei. Their day was still to come.

In spite of the dangerous mountain passes, scarcely wide enough for a truck or cart, I could not help being moved at the sight of the beautiful mountain landscape south of Sian, the majestic Ch'in Ling-shan, the inspiration of so many poets and painters of the past, which we had to traverse on our way into Szechwan. I was surprised to find that the ancient T'ang, Sung and Ming paintings of mountain landscape were not, after all, figments of the artists' imagination. The jagged peaks rose up into the clear air, sometimes shrouded horizontally by little clouds, only to re-emerge again above; and winding paths, sometimes no more than logs driven into the rocks, led through the lower slopes, past little huts and monasteries half hidden by pine trees, just as I had seen them on the scrolls that used to hang on the walls of our house in Peking.

Traveling, either in a passing truck or sometimes on foot along these high mountain passes, was perilous in the extreme. On the steepest slopes, everyone had to get out and push, and many were the trucks that slipped, or skidded, to fall into the abysses below. Gasoline was in desperately short supply, and the saying drummed into every driver was, "One drop of gasoline—one drop of blood." For this reason, trucks had to shut off their engines and coast downhill, with no braking from the low gears, and the descent was correspondingly all the more dangerous. Sixty *li*, or twenty miles, was considered a good average distance to cover in one day. Additional terrors came when one encountered traffic coming the opposite way, as one could never tell what might be around the next bend in the mountain, and the dangers of backing to a passing point were manifest. In the drier weather the continual convoys now sent up clouds of dust as well, which settled on us in a gray cloud.

As we made our way into Szechwan, sometimes getting a lift, sometimes trudging along on foot, occasionally finding a shortcut, along the route through Kwanguan, Kienko and Mienyang, the landscape gradually underwent a transformation. Szechwan is one of the richest, most fertile provinces of China, and it was now, in early June, stiflingly hot. We made our way first to Chengtu, ancient capital of the kingdom of Shu, sixteen hundred years ago, and journeyed southeastward to Chungking, the capital of Szechwan.

Three large rivers cut through the land in deep, straight-sided gorges, so that as one walks along their banks and looks up, the sky looks like a narrow ribbon; and a perpetual mist, caused by the rank heat, hangs over the cliffs. The air is damp and still, but the soil is so fertile that it often bears three or four crops a year, and to own land in Szechwan is to be rich. Many different fruits grow there, including several sorts of orange, such as the thin-skinned *kuang-kan* and the seedless; as well as peaches, apricots, persimmons and pears. Almost everything is grown in Szechwan, from tea in the north and northwest, to corn, wheat, rice, soy beans, and sweet potatoes. All kinds of rare trees are to be found there, a wealth of medicinal herbs, and the largest number of pigs in the whole of China. I could not understand at first what the round, white or bluish-white spots were, continually dipping and bobbing about on the level ground of the fields and hillslopes, until I eventually recognized them as turbans: all the peasants wind cloth around their heads, like Hindus, to protect themselves from the sun and the humidity.

At last, in late June, we reached Chungking, where Generalissimo Chiang Kai-shek had set up his headquarters. I suppose, in some ways, it was the peak moment of his career.

236

Every day I saw people line the streets to watch him pass, and pictures of him and his wife were displayed in every shop window and restaurant. Never again was he to know such popularity, such adulation. Little by little the territory he controlled and the influence he wielded eroded away; first Mongolia, then the disastrous capitulation at Hsüchow, which led eventually to the fall of Nanking, the southern capital, until at last all mainland China passed out of his hands. But all that lay in the unpredictable future, and for the moment he was the idolized leader of Free China.

My sister and I had arrived in Chungking, but our situation was by this time precarious: we had almost completely run out of money, and were lodging in a student hostel that did not provide food. We had imagined it would be easy to find our uncle, General Ting Gin, but no one seemed to know the name. We had not written to him for some years, and we knew no one whatever in Chungking whom we could ask. As the money situation became more pressing, we went out looking for jobs, often losing ourselves in the unfamiliar streets.

One day, on one of these job-hunting expeditions, I noticed a lady on the other side of the street, who began to cross it in our direction, and I remarked to my sister that she looked not unlike my uncle's eldest daughter. The face certainly looked familiar, but we had not seen her for five or six years, and she was much older than we were, with graying hair. Suddenly we recognized one another: it was indeed our first cousin Ting-tsun, who began to question us excitedly, "When did you come?" "Where are you staying?" And we in turn, asked where our uncle lived. She told us the house was only a few blocks away, but she said she must first break it to him gently that we were in Chungking, for he was now over seventy years of age, and she was afraid the sudden news might harm him. She called him first, and then we followed her to the house.

This second family reunion began another flood of questions. My uncle wanted to know where we were staying, and on our telling him we were in a student dormitory, he at once sized up the situation. "That is not good. I know you cannot eat there, you would have to go out for food. You must stay here of course." We were reluctant to give him so much trouble. He had five daughters, all married, whose homes had been overrun by the Communists, and had therefore sought shelter with him. He had one son of college age, and three baby granddaughters, so the household was distinctly crowded. I was overcome by the contrast between my uncle's way of living in Chungking when I recalled the luxury and magnificence he had enjoyed in Peking, but my uncle made light of it. "As one gets older," he said, "one does not need all those fancy things. Now it is a matter of nutrition, not of luxury. This is quite a different way of life; everything is changed, but we are very happy, and optimistic that all will turn out well in the end." And he quoted a favorite slogan of the time: "The final victory is ours." As for our immediate arrangements, he insisted that the children could sleep on the floor if necessary.

My uncle's house, so different from his large and lavishly furnished mansion I had known before in Peking, appeared to us to be a converted office building. Although my uncle had long retired from active service, he had been given a government appointment, so that the lower floor of the wooden, two-storied house was reserved for his offices. The house proper began on the second floor, with many small rooms, very simply furnished; indeed, there was hardly any furniture at all, although naturally many beds, and nothing of elegance anywhere. The repeated bombings had leveled so many houses that people were only too glad to take over office buildings such as this for private dwellings.

There were still many questions to exchange of family

news: my uncle was curious to know how we had fared during the Japanese occupation, and asked what had happened to his house in Peking (it had been taken over by high-ranking Japanese officials) and of course endless questions about our journey. And now we had a wonderful meal, the first good hot meal in Chungking. My aunt—she was in fact my step-aunt, my uncle having remarried after the death of my father's sister—came, unlike the rest of my relations, from an indigenous Peking family, and had been a nurse from quite a modest background. She set a wonderful dinner before us, prepared by her Szechwanese cook. I can still remember what we ate: marinated, salty dried fish; steamed pork (this is very much a home-cooked dish, never encountered in restaurants); and a big sandy pot, into which go long rice noodles, bean curd, Chinese cabbage, some good sorts of ham, and meatballs. It is almost a complete meal in itself, as it has soup, meat and vegetables within the one earthenware pot. We had to sit around two large round tables because there were so many of us, grownups and children, and the delicious food kept on arriving in the center of the table in what seemed to us a never-ending procession, after the privations of the last month.

The Szechwanese chef introduced us to many specialties of his native province in the next few weeks. He had a marvelous way of cooking Szechwan baby corn with pepper and black beans, extremely hot but very good; and *cha-ts'ai*, the roots like turnips, which I had previously known only as pickles and now ate fresh at my uncle's table for the first time.

Gradually the household thinned out a little as my cousins found houses and moved out with their children. My sister and I stayed on, and I found a job teaching Mandarin, or to be quite accurate, two jobs: I taught three students at the American Embassy and six or seven at the Russian Embassy. And then I met my husband, and we were married.

INTERLUDE

Of Leftovers
and the Good Housekeeper

Between the housewife and the head cook in China there could be some differences of opinion. The *ta shih-fu* was apt to buy the best materials, select the best parts of the meat and vegetables, and discard the rest, to the anguish of his mistress, who saw nothing but waste and ruination ahead. My mother exercised great ingenuity in ensuring that food was not thrown away needlessly; and when the Japanese occupation reduced us to the barest rations, her careful husbandry served us in good stead.

The birth of children always meant that we received many red eggs: sometimes as many as twenty or thirty in a basket. My mother's way with these was to shell them, divide them into quarters, put a little oil into a *wok* with a little soy sauce, and stir-fry them quickly until they were browned a little on the outside. They were then served for breakfast as an accompaniment to *hsi-fan* (congee).

Pao-ping, the wheaten pancakes of northern China, became very hard and dry in a short time, but could be restored to life and new use by slicing them into strips and adding them to chicken broth, to become an economical form of soup noodle. And they served a purpose, too, when added to a meat and vegetable dish which needed extending a little.

If by some chance half of a fish was left over, one could add it to some good soup, along with some bean curd, and produce, with the aid of a little soy sauce, an attractive dish called *yü-shao tou-fu*.

Sauce from red-cooking was always treasured and kept, and always improved with age. Some restaurants were famous for their sauces, reputedly started fifty or a hundred years ago. I have been told that the solera system of making sherry embodies the same principle. Chinese cabbage tasted delicious when stir-fried in sauce left over from red-cooked pork; and if one added vegetables and meat to leftover noodles, one had a very passable *ch'ao mien!* Prawns Szechwan also produced much sauce, to which bean curd could be added to make yet another attractive dish.

With a little imagination, rice can be used with leftover dishes or converted to something new. Rice itself cannot be reheated, but one can add some fresh eggs to it and some leftover Chinese sausage, then stir-fry the mixture in a little oil, and you have produced *ch'ao-fan*. One can also add water to cooked rice and produce *p'ao-fan*, something between congee and dry rice, which goes well with leftovers of most kinds.

Hsi-fan, the thin gruel eaten with pickles and other savory dishes at breakfast and at midnight, is particularly good with any remainders, and is unbelievably simple to make. For the rice usually served you need one level rice-bowlful for four people, and you put it into a pot with two fingers width of water above the rice. Start at high heat, until it approaches the boil, then lower, and cook covered until the rice softens. With congee, or *hsi-fan*, you need only one-third of a bowl of rice to two quarts of water, which you keep boiling until the rice is soft. The best rice for congee, oddly enough, is the semi-glutinous kind which is grown near my mother's birthplace, in the Wu-hsi region of lower Kiangsu province.

My mother frequently made too many *chiao-tzu*, the dumplings stuffed in Peking mainly with lamb or pork, particularly the kind known as *shui-chiao*, "water" dumplings. If there were many left over, she speedily turned them into *kuo-t'ieh*, sometimes translated as "pot-stickers" because one cooks them first of all in a pan brushed lightly with vegetable oil, and arranges them in it so that they do not touch. You then add a cup of water and cook them covered until the water evaporates—about five minutes. The underside of these crescent-shaped dumplings has been turned meanwhile to a golden brown. These are perfectly delicious eaten hot after being dipped in a little pepper oil and Chinese vinegar: one bites through the covering and encounters the juicy meat, or meat and vegetable filling. In southern China prawns, shrimp, ginger and other ingredients could be added to the filling to make yet another version.

Chiao-tzu, originally a northern Chinese preparation, eaten particularly at the New Year, but also pleasant to nibble on at morning, afternoon or late-night snacks, are quite well adapted for serving as *hors d'oeuvre*, although they need a certain amount of skill in the making. This recipe shows the *chiao-tzu* as prepared in the south. In Peking the filling was of lamb or pork exclusively, and in Szechwan one also found cabbage. The shrimp are a Cantonese touch.

STUFFED DUMPLINGS
CHIAO-TZU

4 cups all-purpose flour
1½ cups cold water

FILLING
½ cup finely chopped
  cooked shrimp

1 cup (scant) finely chopped
  lean raw pork
1⅓ cups finely chopped
  fresh raw Chinese
  cabbage

Prepare the filling first. Discard the outer leaves of the cabbage, and after chopping the rest, squeeze in a kitchen cloth to extract as much moisture as possible. Mix the cabbage in a bowl with the pork and shrimp, and store in the refrigerator for one hour to firm up and blend the flavors. The quantity will be sufficient for one hundred dumplings, or about eight dozen.

Combine the flour with the water gradually, starting with half the water, and mixing well. Knead the dough on a lightly floured board until completely smooth, and then allow it to rest for about twenty minutes, varying the time with the heat of the kitchen.

Now put the dough on a lightly floured board and roll it into a long roll about one and a half inches in diameter. Cut into one-inch rounds, sprinkle each round lightly with flour, and flatten on the table with the ball of the hand; then roll out into a three-inch circle, turning the dough at each roll of the pin. Place a scant tablespoonful of the filling into the center of each round. Do not overfill, or the *chiao-tzu* will break open. Lay the *chiao-tzu* in the curve made by the base of the fingers and the palm of the hand, and with your other hand bring the central portions of the dough together. Then crimp the dough together from either end, with the seam thus made uppermost, and the bottom slightly flattened, to make a plump, crescent-shaped dumpling. You may now add the *chiao-tzu* to chicken stock if you like, and you will then have delicious soup dumplings.

More difficult, although well worth the trouble, is the method which transforms *chiao-tzu* into *kuo-t'ieh;* and these can be added to one's repertoire for cocktail parties.

GRILLED POT STICKERS
KUO-T'IEH

Heat two to three tablespoons of vegetable oil to high heat in a warmed skillet, and lay the *chiao-tzu* flat side down in rows, making sure they do not touch one another. Add one and a half cups of water, cover, and cook for five to six minutes. The underside of the *kuo-t'ieh* should be nicely browned and crisp, the sides moistly steamed and the filling piping hot. Serve immediately, and provide a saucer in which to mix a dipping sauce of hot pepper oil (see page 161) and Chinese vinegar according to individual tastes; and a little soy sauce may be added if it is liked.

PRAWNS SZECHWAN
KAN-SHAO MING-HSIA

½ pound uncooked prawns
½ teaspoon minced garlic
½ teaspoon grated ginger root
2 tablespoons chopped scallions
1 teaspoon finely chopped dried red chili peppers
2 tablespoons vegetable oil

2 tablespoons Chinese rice wine or dry sherry
1 tablespoon catsup
pinch of sugar
1 teaspoon cornstarch mixed with 2 tablespoons water
3 drops sesame seed oil (optional)

Heat a *wok*, add the oil, and bring to high heat. Stir-fry the prawns, garlic, ginger root, scallions and chili peppers for two minutes, and then add the rice wine, followed by the cornstarch-and-water mixture, and continue rapidly stirring and tossing until the shrimp are done. They should be pink and have a crunchy texture. The sesame seed oil is added now, if desired, and the shrimp given a last toss to incorporate the flavor.

Since Chinese dishes are not served swimming in sauce, the surplus should be kept, and used as a base for other dishes. As I have mentioned, some bean curd can be cooked in this highly flavored sauce, as an attractive side dish; and one can use one's ingenuity in devising variations and embellishments. Imagination is the sign of the good cook around the world.

TWELFTH MOON

ALTHOUGH MY UNCLE, General Ting Gin, and his daughters naturally attended my wedding since I was married from his house, it was an event singularly lacking in relatives. Both my husband's family and mine were almost all in the north, in or near Peking, or otherwise scattered by the troubled times and unable to be present. Nevertheless, I began to form an impression that my husband's maternal grandfather must have had an unusually romantic disposition: two relatives, entirely unknown to either of us, appeared for the ceremonies, one of whom announced himself as my husband's thirty-ninth uncle, and the other, as his twenty-eighth. My father-in-law, as I was also to learn, had had twelve wives, so that uxoriousness seemed to be typical of both his ancestral lines.

Relationships were always a trifle complicated in China, as multiple wives and concubines were the rule and custom; and it was not uncommon for the Number One wife to keep the children of secondary wives and arrange for most of the supernumerary mothers to be cast out. If most Chinese wives were amiable, others were ruthless in the face of competition: and an effective method to prevent a spouse from straying was to coax him into smoking opium, which reduced his interest in outside amorous activities and kept him of necessity at home. Since the preparation of his jade and ivory pipe was a delicate operation, the wife saw to it that a beautiful young maidservant was always at hand for this purpose, one who could at the same time watch over all his movements. My father-in-law, as I later found out, was an opium smoker.

In my own family I never really knew the full extent of the ramifications of our kith and kin, and if I ever inquired about some obscure connection or cousin who appeared at the house, my mother would reprimand me sharply for asking impertinent questions, which effectually silenced my curiosity. A genealogical tree was carefully maintained in a book, written in brush characters, but I do not recollect ever paying much attention to it.

With marriage I returned to most of the comforts of my Peking life: a houseful of servants, a good cook, and all the amenities to which I had been accustomed. Chungking itself was in other respects decidedly provincial and behind the times. The distinctive cuisine of Szechwan of course interested me, with its hot, peppery and spicy foods. One unusual dish I encountered in this province is probably not likely to recommend itself to Western palates: the *mao tu k'ai tung*, a highly spiced firepot, in which beef tripe is the principal ingredient, accompanied by a special black sauce, which is perpetually maintained, sometimes for as long as ten years. It is quite an esoteric experience to go into a dark little restaurant in Chengtu and dip the pieces of tripe, served in an ancient, blackened iron pot, into the still more ancient sauce, and eat it over a bowl of steamed white rice. Chungking, the capital, was renowned for its street vendors, who set up little tents in the open, anchored to the ground with large stones, and called out the delicacies they served. Hot *hsi-fan*, or, alternatively, cold noodles; *lü-tou*, the shucks of young peas dipped in sugar; sliced cold meats and little pickled vegetables (*p'ao-ts'ai*) were among the most popular items, and tent after tent had a rough wooden table and a bench outside it for the hungry passer-by to pause and refresh himself.

After a while, as V-J Day approached, we decided to move to Shanghai, where my younger brother was living, and we presently established ourselves there. The move gave me the first opportunity I had ever had to visit the land whence my parents had come, Wu-hsi, with its silk factories and flour mills, smiling countryside and delicious food. I also saw at last the exquisitely lovely T'ai Hu, the lake of which my mother always spoke with nostalgia.

We went to Wu-hsi by train, with my brother and my sister-in-law (my brother at that time owned a celebrated restaurant in Shanghai, in the Park Hotel), and saw the shattered remains of my parents' house, destroyed by the Japanese, and the garden, overgrown with weeds. I saw the tombs of my ancestors at Wu-li Ts'un, "Five Mile Village," at its beautiful site on a gentle rise, sheltered by trees and overlooking the water, all carefully planned by my forebears in consultation with the geomancer, for the most auspicious placement and aspect.

On one memorable evening, at the time of the August Moon, my brother arranged a boat banquet, *ch'uan-ts'ai*, on the T'ai Hu. Opera singers and musicians accompanied us, and a chef from my brother's restaurant, and all the fish for the dinner came from the lake, carried alive in wicker baskets until the time for preparing the meal. The moon rode serenely in the clear sky and was reflected in the water, and the company recited and composed poems; the sound of laughter and applause carried across the lake as dusk wore on into night.

The dinner lasted the entire evening, and was served in an endless procession of dishes, with a fresh plate for each course, to the accompaniment of music and singing. I am grateful to have known moments like that water-borne party on the T'ai Hu, which I am afraid have gone forever, grateful that I have known the best of that vanished world: and yet, but for the war, and that rash enthusiasm that carried me out of Peking into almost a different century, I would never have known that I could work, and support two children, and carve a career for myself in a new country. Most of my contemporaries, I feel, did not have an opportunity of living a full life: if I myself remember the past with gratitude, it is also without regret. Happy as I was in the Peking of my childhood, I could never have returned to that formal pattern after my eyes had been opened by experience of other ways and other freedoms. And yet I had not been wholly unprepared for a new life: my parents' example and my own predilections had always made me interested in people, interested in new things, ready to tackle any difficulty—and I had never formed any bad habits of laziness or indifference.

Shanghai was quite unlike Peking. Shanghai had every kind of amusement, and a night life from twilight to dawn. Peking was very much the historic capital, whereas in Shanghai I found myself in a sophisticated modern city. In Shanghai, as in Tientsin, restaurants opened at four in the morning, serving cold-tossed noodles, with cold cucumber, chicken, sesame seed paste, Chinese parsley, and ham, as well as drinks, for a restorative snack after dancing. These restaurants were especially the resort of nightclub girls, who did not eat during the day, and were taken out after the show by the patrons of the clubs. Dance hostesses at the clubs used to receive one dollar for three dances, and if a guest wished to prolong the evening, he might have to pay as much as a hundred dollars —but it depended very much on whether the hostess found her partner agreeable. Captains circulated anxiously around the tables, checking on the tips the girls received, since they received a percentage of the amount as part of their earnings. Some of the best restaurants in Shanghai also stayed open late, particularly the fine French ones; in Peking, the limited night life was confined for the most part to the Legation Quarter, to such places as the Wagon-Lit Hotel, the German Hotel, and the Grand Hôtel de Pékin.

Our life in Shanghai was conducted on an elaborate scale, which now included a racing stable; the horses were chiefly of mixed blood lines, half Japanese and half Australian. I found riding on them a very different experience from a comfortable hack on our sure-footed little Peking ponies. The racehorses started out amiably enough, but they soon settled into an unmanageable stride whenever one turned towards home, and could not be diverted from going back to the stables by the shortest route they knew.

In the winter of 1946 we received word by telegram that my husband's grandmother was dying. She was eighty-six years old and knew that the end was near, but had sent word that she would not close her eyes until she had seen her Number One grandson, who had always been her favorite. We set out accordingly by plane for Peking. It was a time of appalling winter storms: two planes of previous flights had crashed, and we were naturally apprehensive of a third disaster. As we neared the capital we ran into a flurry of snow, which had a magical effect on the whole city, and there was an extraordinary moment when the golden roofs of the palace peered through the driving flakes and confirmed that we had arrived at the Forbidden City.

We had arranged that we should go first to my parents, with whom we were planning to stay, but as our flight had been long delayed by the weather, they did not know when we were coming, and when we drew up in a taxi at the house, they were not expecting us. We went, naturally, to the main gates, as was only fitting in introducing my husband to my family, but when we rang, there was no answer. It slowly dawned on me that the front part of the house, which had been divided off by the Japanese, was not occupied by the family any more; we went back to the cab, and turned about to go to the small rear door which opened into the house from the parallel street behind it. Here was a fresh shock. The servant who opened the door was an unknown face and did not recognize me, and we were left in the cutting wind while he went to fetch someone from inside to identify us. I was horrified to see my father appear at the door, when we should have gone to him—much had changed in my absence. My mother, I noticed, had aged, like my father, as a result of the privations of the occupation, and was growing deaf. Only the last two rows of pavilions and courtyards remained in use. In our large kitchen, with its long line of stoves, there was now only one. Some of the older servants had died, some had gone away; and there remained only two and a rickshaw boy. The rooms were bare and cold, and I was saddened and shocked at the transformation.

My husband went to see his grandmother, and true to her word, she remained conscious long enough to recognize him, and soon afterwards died, and we attended her funeral. She had devoted herself to my husband; he was the apple of her eye, and when he first went to grammar school, at the age of six, she used to carry his books for him. He had been waited on hand and foot: a contemporary of his told me that at first he was also accompanied to school by a servant carrying his chamber pot, in case he should have a little weakness that boys are prone to, on the way or while in class. His grandmother's joy and pride had increased throughout his school years. He had been a brilliant student—always first, with straight A's in high school and in college, justifying her feelings for him, which had been little short of adoration.

Although my husband and I had never known one another in Peking, a strange linkage between us arose from an incident of my own college days. During my last years at the Bridgeman Academy we were visited by an old lady in her sixties, who lectured to us on the Boxer Rebellion. She had been a celebrated personage in her time, and still had a delightful manner and personality, petite, with the tiny bound feet of her generation. She was Sai Chin-hua, born in Kiangsu of a good but not wealthy family. Her charm and good looks had led her to become a prostitute of distinction. I qualify the word purposely: "prostitute" does not convey the respected place ladies of this kind occupied in old China, and they were not regarded, as in the West, as merely the subject of sordid commercial transactions; and being intelligent, accomplished and well-bred, they often married people of position.

At the time of the Boxer Rebellion, when the Empress-Dowager Tz'u-hsi had fled to Sian, and the eight European powers had taken over Peking, Sai Chin-hua had won the affections of the German general in command of his country's forces, but had refused to accede to his attentions. When, however, she saw the dreadful destruction of Yüan-ming Yüan, the favorite palace of Tz'u-hsi, she gave way and said she would grant him anything he asked if he would stop the excesses of the soldiery. He agreed to do whatever he could, and offered to install her in the Imperial Palace, saying she could have anything she wished in it. Sai Chin-hua would have nothing of this, and told the general that everything belonged to the ruling dynasty and it was wrong that its possessions should be used by anyone else. (The Summer Palace was, of course, looted by the Allied troops, to its almost complete destruction, and its treasures scattered all over Europe: Queen Victoria acquired one of the Pekinese found in the Imperial apartments, and named it, in somewhat questionable taste, "Looty.") Sai Chin-hua eventually became the mistress of the German general. After the general returned to Germany, she later married one of the richest men in China. This man became what is known as a "dry" brother, *kan-ti*, of my father-in-law, that is to say, they had gone through various formal rites, including the exchange of their horoscopes, and become brothers by declaration, although not by blood, at a party of recognition. Sai Chin-hua thus became my husband's "dry" aunt and godmother, or *kan-ma*. I never met her after my marriage, for she was by that time old and ill, and the family visited her only rarely and sent her small gifts. She had become poor, almost destitute, but she would have lost face if she had asked her relations for money. Women of her position knew nothing of finance or investments: they used what they had until it was all spent. Sadly, she had also become addicted to opium. She died on her opium couch, alone except for one old maidservant still faithful to her. I visited her tomb in Peking, which was at a beautiful place and had become a tourist attraction, for her patriotism at the time of the Boxer Rebellion had not been forgotten.

My Number One, Two and Three sisters had by this time returned to Peking, so that we had something of a family reunion. My Number Two sister's husband had become a professor on the staff of Tsing Hua University; and in the full confidence of my married state, I no longer found her, or my other elder sisters, as alarming as I had when a child.

I delighted in rediscovering the city once again. I explored the Summer Palace, the Temple of Heaven, and Pei Hai Park, as well as all the pullulating bazaars, like the Lung-fu Szu (Prosperity and Good Luck Temple), the finest of them all, overflowing with silks and jewels at the time of the new and the full moon (at the New Year, the merchants even used to borrow particularly magnificent objects, purely for display), and one could often find a good bargain there. At the Liu-li Ch'ang, or "Ceramic Factory," whose name harked back to earlier times, when it had been the locality for porcelains, one found all the bookstores, stocked with the old classics, as well as modern publications; and the narrow lanes still remained, devoted to scissors, furs, silks, fans, jade, embroidery, and Peking glass. Each had a separate alley to itself.

At T'ien Ch'iao, "Heaven's Bridge," near the Ch'ien Men,

or "Front Gate," the dealers in stolen goods still foregathered at dawn, and one had to be wary of pickpockets. T'ien Ch'iao was also famous for its acrobats: one kind wore an outfit with a mask and counterfeited the antics of two men wrestling, making the crowds chuckle; and the real wrestlers, comedians in their own right, talked and quipped with the people gathered around, and would not begin until they had judged that the bystanders had thrown enough money on the ground to make it worth their while. This bantering foreshow gave rise to a common saying (which I still use sometimes, although few understand me any more), "You are a T'ien Ch'iao acrobat," which, being interpreted, means, "You do a lot of talking—why don't you go ahead and do it!"

We stayed in Peking for about four months, leaving at the most beautiful season of the year, the Fourth Moon, with the spring flowers still in blossom. I bade farewell to my parents once again, in a quite different frame of mind from our last parting, never dreaming that this was to be a much more decisive break, and that I should never see them again. We returned to Shanghai, where we lived until 1949, when my husband was appointed commercial attaché to the Chinese Mission in Japan. We left together on what proved to be the last plane out of Shanghai; but although Nanking, Chiang Kai-shek's last capital in mainland China, had already fallen, everyone still voiced optimistic sentiments, from the Generalissimo downwards, and we had no conception that it would be impossible to return.

My course, from the moment I left Peking, had been toward America, although even at that time I had no idea in what direction I was ultimately to travel. One part of my life had vanished: a new part was opening before me. I had never been afraid of the future, and I looked forward to it eagerly.

TWO POSTSCRIPTS

Practical Shopping

Although exploring for ingredients used in a Chinese kitchen in an American city is certainly different from what I knew in China, it is still not the same as the American housewife's pattern. She can find almost all she wants in a supermarket, but if I were taking a friend, for instance, on a shopping expedition in San Francisco's Chinatown, we would follow a quite different route.

Unlike Peking, San Francisco's Chinese shops are confined to a comparatively limited area. They cluster along Grant Avenue and Stockton Street, and the intervening cross-streets. Instead of the lanes of Peking devoted to one kind of merchandise only, every type of shop, from the seller of silks to the antique dealer in ancient porcelains, is to be found cheek by jowl; and in general, in the United States, wherever a substantial body of Chinese citizens are found, the shopping area is usually conveniently compact. This is an advantage, as one still has to go to individual shops for most categories of merchandise.

It is certainly much easier now than a few years ago to find the spices and seasonings one needs, and this must be directly attributable to the increased interest in Chinese cooking; but one must still know where to go to buy what one wants.

For the actual implements used in the kitchen it is hardly necessary to go to Chinatown: they are to be found at almost all big stores. The basic requirements are as follows:

> A chopping block
> 2 *wok* each with a lid (*wok* is the Cantonese name;
>   in Mandarin it is *kuo-tzu*)
> 1 or 2 Chinese cleavers
> 1 Chinese bamboo steamer
> 2 pairs of long, cooking chopsticks
> 1 large cooking ladle
> 1 strainer
> 1 spatula

Without these implements it would be pointless to set out on a shopping expedition preparatory to cooking a Chinese meal; whereas with them you have all the tools of a Chinese cook—leaving aside such considerations as the pots you need for the Mongolian firepot, or a smoke oven for smoked tea duck.

If we begin at the butcher's shop, we find fresh meats, but also bacon and ham, and a number of preserved foods, such as salty eggs, salty ham, salty duck feet, preserved dried duck, Chinese sausages, and salty pressed fish; there are even a few vegetables.

Grouped together at the fishmonger's, in addition to fresh fish, crab and other seafood, are chicken and duck, and in some instances one finds limited amounts of meat. It is not unusual to find that some of the fish are swimming in quite a lively way in a tank, to be chosen for size and appearance by the customers.

The greengrocer's shop stocks both vegetables and fruits. In San Francisco these provisions are set out on display carts, wheeled outside the shop to attract passersby, a practice of questionable legality, but one more honored in the breach than the observance. At such shops I look for the freshest Chinese cabbage and squash; winter melon, for soup; hairy melon (immediately identifiable by its shaggy appearance);

and seasonal vegetables, such as cucumber and eggplant. Apart from the green vegetables, Chinese chard and snow peas, one finds lotus seed and lotus root (which has numerous uses), water chestnuts, and taro root, which is much preferred to potatoes in Peking.

The dry grocery shops in Chinatown are the source of such staples as tea in cans or packages, although it can be said that not more than a fraction of the some two hundred and fifty varieties of tea are available. Rice and flour of several kinds are stocked as well; and such important farinaceous items as fresh noodles; fresh *wonton* skin; fresh bean curd; imported soy sauce, both light and dark, in differing grades; Chinese vinegar; and cooking wine. Noodles and *wonton* can be prepared in the kitchen, but it is a great saver of time to buy them already prepared.

A distinct innovation is the appearance of the cooked-food shop. In China, there is a long tradition of eating food prepared in the street, from dawn to nightfall, but at these new-style shops you can buy the ready-to-eat components of a complete meal to take home. Naturally, the system is defeated by the nature of some Chinese dishes, which do not take kindly to reheating, but the range is nevertheless wide. I have seen the following dishes set out to entice the housewife short of time:

Roast Duck	Roast Turkey
Roast Chicken	Roast Pig
Curried Crab	Roast Ham
Sweet-Sour Pork	Pork Stomach
Barbecued Spareribs	Winter Melon
lo-han ts'ai (a Buddhist eight precious vegetable dish)	Chinese Squash
	Oyster Sauce Bean Curd
	Black Mushrooms
Barbecued Pork Sautéed with Eggs	Ginkgo Nuts
	Pressed Bean Curd
Red-cooked Chicken	Roast Squab
Sweet-Sour Pigs Feet	

At such food shops one usually finds a selection of Oriental and Occidental pastries and cakes as well, although, for choice, one might prefer to go to the specialized bakeries.

Since the shops in San Francisco's Chinatown are predominantly Cantonese, one finds a considerable variety of real Chinese sweet tea pastries and tea cakes. The pastries have a delicate, short crust, made with lard, and with fillings such as bean paste and lotus root paste; and moon cakes, richly stuffed with fruits, are to be found in and out of season. Curry puffs and assorted *pao*, the Cantonese term for the Mandarin *ping*, stuffed with barbecued pork, *har gao* (shrimp), as well as sweet fillings, and glutinous rice sweetmeats are offered. Western-style cakes, pies and cupcakes, are also made at the bakeries, which combine these with preserved fruits, kumquats, melon and coconut in crystalized sugar, either separately or as appropriate gifts in special boxes for the New Year.

For special seasonings I make my way to an herb shop, although some are still hard to come by. The essentials, such as five-spice powder (a combination of anise seed, fennel, clove, cinnamon bark and Szechwan peppercorns ground together) are obtained there, as well as individual measures of Szechwan peppercorns and five-star anise.

The dry goods store provides me with pressed bean curd and bean curd sheets, dried mushrooms, fungus such as silver ear and dried tiger lily buds (golden needles) on the one hand, and thousand-year eggs, bird's nests, sea cucumber (*bêche-de-mer*), and shark fin, on the other. The quality of the last group may vary considerably; one must have a standard of judgment for the last three and a long purse as well. Because many Chinese restaurants serve inexpensive food, there has arisen the erroneous conception that Chinese food is less costly than Western. It needs only a brief inspection of the price of such items as the best-quality bird's nest or shark fin, or a consideration of the long, patient hours spent in the preparation of the dishes of which they form part, to furnish a rebuttal.

The following stores will fill mail orders for ingredients for Chinese cooking:

Eastern Trading Company
2801 Broadway
New York, N.Y. 10013

Wing Sing Chong Company
1076 Stockton Street
San Francisco, Calif. 94108

Yuit Hing Market Corpora-
tion
23 Pell Street
New York, N.Y. 10013

Cheong-Leen Supermarket
Tower House
4-10 Tower Street
London, W.C. 2, England

Tuck Cheong & Company
617 H Street, N.W.
Washington, D.C. 20001

Glossary of Regional Methods
of Preparing Chinese Food

In the China of my youth the regional differences of Chinese cuisine were strongly marked. I had the personal advantage of being, in the proverbial phrase, *nan-sheng pei-chang,* "southern-born, northern-reared," and fortunate enough to know the full variety of the dishes of the "Middle Kingdom," *Chung-kuo,* from an early period. Traveling across China widened my experience at first hand. It seems likely that improved communications in mainland China may eventually obscure these local differences; and certainly one encounters abroad a blunting of the individual peaks of Chinese cooking by chefs who feel impelled to modify the classic preparations of China in deference to the tastes of the country of their adoption.

It was not only the kinds of food that differed, or the bland versus the spicy, but the actual cooking methods in different provinces. I think the following list of some twenty-three distinct methods of preparing food is therefore not without interest.

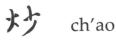 ch'ao   Quick stir-frying over high heat in an uncovered *wok,* with little oil. "To sauté" is the nearest equivalent. Universal

溜	liu	Quick stir-frying over low heat in an uncovered *wok,* with more oil than in *ch'ao.* Northern China
煎	chien	Shallow-frying.
烤	k'ao	Roasting (for example, a pig) or broiling. More or less identical with *hung* below. Canton
烘	hung	"Baking." Northern
蒸	cheng	Steaming. Universal
燉	tun	Stewing, in a covered pot (soupy in style, as in chicken or beef stew). Shanghai
燴	hui	Stewing, in a covered pot but for a shorter time than in *tun.* Shanghai and northern
熬	ao	Simmering, covered, with less liquid than in *chu* below. For seafood. Peking
煮	chu	Simmering, covered. Northern and southern
炸	cha	Deep-frying. Universal
拌	pan	Cold-tossing of vegetables like cucumber, or of cold chicken in summer. Northern

溜	chün	Plunging rapidly in and out of hot oil. Northern
燒	shao	Stewing with soy sauce, as in "red-cooking" (*hung-shao*). Universal
燜	men	Simmering over low heat, covered. Northern
烹	p'eng	Splashing, as when seasoning is "splashed" over food for a few seconds in deep-frying. Northern
涮	shuan	Rinsing, as when lamb is swung to and fro in a firepot as though being "rinsed" in the liquid. Northern
爆	p'ao	Braising, as in cooking lamb in very hot oil—in and out. Northern
滷	lu	Simmering slowly with soy sauce, as in five-spiced beef (*lu-shui:* sauce). Northern style tends to be salty; southern, sweeter.
薰	hsün	Smoking, of fish, pork or duck. Northern
煸	pien	Dry and quick stir-frying without oil or sauce. Strictly Szechwan
淹	yen	Soaking or steeping, as in *p'ao-ts'ai,* Szechwan steeped vegetables. Szechwan
烙	lao	Dry grilling, as in cooking wheat-flour cakes in a skillet without oil. Northern

INDEX OF RECIPES